Haunted
Tennessee

Ghosts and Strange Phenomena
of the Volunteer State

Alan Brown

Illustrations by Heather Adel Wiggins

STACKPOLE
BOOKS

To my daughter Andrea and my son-in-law Kenny,
who have given me another reason to love Memphis

Copyright © 2009 by Stackpole Books

Published in 2009 by
STACKPOLE BOOKS
5067 Ritter Road
Mechanicsburg, PA 17055
www.stackpolebooks.com

Printed in the United States of America

FIRST EDITION

Cover design by Caroline Stover

Library of Congress Cataloging-in-Publication Data

Brown, Alan, 1950 Jan. 12-
    Haunted Tennessee : ghosts and strange phenomena of the volunteer state / by Alan Brown ; illustrations by Heather Adel Wiggins.
        p.   cm.
    Includes bibliographical references.
    ISBN-13: 978-0-8117-3540-7 (pbk.)
    ISBN-10: 0-8117-3540-0 (pbk.)
    1. Ghosts—Tennessee. 2. Haunted places—Tennessee. I. Title.
BF1472.U6B7435   2009
133.109768—dc22

                                                        2008040678

Contents

Introduction

TENNESSEE IS A MULTIFACETED STATE, WITH LARGE CITIES AND SMALL towns; mountains, forests, and fields; and rivers and lakes. Tennessee is known as the "Volunteer State," for the large number of soldiers the state provided during the War of 1812 and the Mexican War, but from a historical perspective, it is also, as the Cherokee chief Dragging Canoe put it, the "Dark and Bloody Ground." Ghosts seem to be found everywhere in Tennessee, from the bucolic small towns to the weathered historic districts of its metropolitan centers. Tennessee is indeed a haunted state.

Tennessee's storied past is populated by a number of iconic figures, many of whom are now said to haunt the places where they once lived or visited. Andrew Jackson, they say, made a return visit to his beloved Hermitage toward the end of the nineteenth century. Jackson also plays a prominent role in what has become one of Tennessee's—and America's—greatest ghost stories: that of the Bell Witch. Patrick Cleburne, one of the Confederate generals who fell at the Battle of Franklin, can still be seen standing on the porch where his body was placed awaiting burial. Hank Williams, the undisputed king of country-western music, is said to haunt the Ryman Auditorium, where he performed for the Grand Ole Opry. If the photographic evidence can be believed, Elvis Presley can still be seen staring out of one of the second-floor windows of Graceland. Strong personalities, it seems, tend to make a lasting impression on the landscape.

The majority of Tennessee's ghosts apparently emerged from the conflicts that left their bloody imprint on the history of the state.

The ghosts of Cherokee, Choctaw, and Chickasaw Indians who perished aiding the British in the Revolutionary War and fighting the settlers in the nineteenth century stride proudly through many of the state's oldest and most enduring legends. Many soldiers who died in some of the most horrible battles of the Civil War, such as Shiloh, Stones River, and Franklin, are believed to haunt many of the antebellum homes that were converted into makeshift hospitals. And it seems that some of the most dedicated spirits are still at their posts, defending old forts and standing watch in the trenches of the battlefields. Even country music legend Loretta Lynn's mansion in Hurricane Mills is reputed to be haunted by the Confederate soldiers buried on her property.

Some of Tennessee's most moving ghost stories focus more on personal misfortunes, however. The tragically premature deaths of little Nina Craigmiles in a carriage accident and wealthy Adelicia Acklen's infant twins have generated ghost stories that are just as likely to evoke tears as goose bumps. The suicides that are memorialized in the campus lore of many of Tennessee's colleges and universities remind us that simply growing up and living on one's own can be too daunting a task for some young people.

Tennessee's rugged terrain is also said to be home to some mysterious creatures. In the colorfully named Suck Lick Creek and Flintville, a Bigfoot-like being has been seen loping through the foothills. In October 1950, a number of UFOs reportedly streaked through the night skies of Oak Ridge. And a half-human, half-feline creature called the Wampus Cat has stalked through the nightmares of Native Americans and residents of the region for generations. Ghosts, it appears, are not the only fearsome beings in Tennessee.

If the preceding paragraphs have not convinced you that Dragging Canoe was correct when he called Tennessee the Dark and Bloody Ground, read on. I think you will find that the old Cherokee chief's pronouncement was more accurate than he ever realized.

Central Tennessee

CENTRAL TENNESSEE LIES IN THE HEART OF THE NASHVILLE BASIN, or Central Basin, which drains toward the northwest. The region includes Nashville, the state capital and second largest city in Tennessee. The basin is also an agricultural region whose rolling meadows and fertile fields have made it one of the wealthiest parts of the state.

Bigfoot, the Man-Beast

Until the 1970s, Bigfoot, or Sasquatch, was considered by most people to be a quasimythical beast that inhabited the great forests of Oregon, Washington, and California. In 1972, the release of *The Legend of Boggy Creek*, a low-budget docudrama about Arkansas's Fouke Monster, forever altered the nation's perception of the giant humanoid creature. People were now ready to believe what Southerners had known all along: that Bigfoot-like monsters have been sighted south of the Mason-Dixon line for years. And Tennessee is one of the Southern states reputedly home to Bigfoot.

One of the first reported sightings of Bigfoot took place in the spring of 1974 along South Lick Creek Road in Williamson County. Two boys were riding their minibikes out in the country, looking for bait to go fishing. They parked their bikes on the roadside and

walked down a path toward a pasture where cattle were grazing. After a few minutes, one of the brothers began to feel uncomfortable. He sensed that he and his brother were being watched. Suddenly the boys stopped dead in their tracks. Off to their left, approximately forty yards from the main road, was a hairy, manlike creature. It was crouching in a small patch of mayapples, raking its arms along the ground. The animal saw the two boys but did not appear to be disturbed by their presence. Later, the boys described the creature as standing between five and six feet high, with medium brown hair, a low gorillalike head, and long arms. Terrified, the boys ran away as fast their legs could carry them, slowing down just long enough to glance over their shoulder at the monster, which continued picking around the patch of mayapples.

Several even more frightening incidents reportedly took place in Flintville, about seven miles west of Chattanooga. For more than twenty years, residents of Flintville were terrified by a beast that carried off livestock and left behind sixteen-inch footprints and a pungent odor. One man swore that a seven-foot monster chased him through the woods, screaming and howling. In 1976, a frantic woman told police that a "giant, hairy monster" pounced onto the roof of her car and jumped up and down. It also broke off the car's antenna. That same year, Jennie Robertson was doing housework while her four-year-old son, Gary, was playing outside. She immediately stopped what she was doing when she heard him scream. As Jennie ran outside, her nostrils were assailed by a terrible odor that reminded her of dead rats. Then she saw something that caused chills to run up her spine. A seven- or eight-foot beast that was covered with hair was loping across the yard toward her son. Just before the monster grabbed Gary, Jennie scooped up the frightened child in her arms and ran back inside the house. While she locked the doors, she noticed that the creature had melted into the woods. She called the police and, in a trembling voice, reported her son's near abduction. The police spent most of the night combing the woods for the creature, which screamed if they got too close and threw rocks at them. The sixteen-inch footprints the police found the next morning convinced them that the woman had had an actual encounter with Bigfoot.

In the 1980s, police received a number of reports of Bigfoot attacks. A plumber complained that a hairy monster had destroyed the windshield of his truck. A group of teenagers told police that they saw some sort of man-beast shambling across a field. In 1989, a preacher reported that a creature had broken the antenna and windshield of his car.

In nearby Rutherford County, near the Walter Hill community, a couple of hikers were walking through the woods in 1987 when something standing on the other side of a clearing caught their attention. Walking in front of a stand of pine trees was a six-and-a-half- to seven-and-a-half-foot tall creature they described as a Sasquatch. The monster went on its way, seemingly oblivious to the hikers. Later, while searching the area about a quarter mile from their house, the hikers found large tracks, bedding sites, and branches that appeared to have had the leaves eaten off them.

After 1993, no more sightings were reported for several years. Then in the early 2000s, a woman named Janice Coy contacted a group of Bigfoot investigators regarding a creature that had been going into the basement of her farmhouse. One of the researchers, Mary Green, stayed outside with the camera running. Later, when Mary reviewed the film, she was surprised to find that she had accidentally photographed a creature at the bottom of a hill. She then recalled that she had heard a strange grunting sound while she was filming. In the controversial film, which Mary Green posted on cryptozoology.com, you can see what could be a head in the grass. Skeptics have pointed out, however, that the "face" is too blurry to identify positively as belonging to a Bigfoot. Until a higher-resolution file shows up on the Internet, the Bigfoot of Central Tennessee will remain an intriguing legend, and nothing more.

Chapel Hill's Ghost Light

Ghost lights have been an integral part of the folklore of the West and South for centuries. Witnesses have described these anomalies as glowing balls or balls of lights, some of which emitted all the colors of the rainbow, while others had only one or two colors. Ghost lights have been said to sparkle, to move or remain stationary, to hover over the ground or soar high into the night sky. Ghost lights have been called earthlights, spooklights, and will-o'-the-wisps. In Tennessee, the most famous ghost light is that attributed to the phantom signalman of Chapel Hill.

On the surface, the legend of the phantom signalman seems to be a generic version of the classic railroad ghost story. Some time around the late 1800s or early 1900s, Chapel Hill was a whistle-stop on the Louisville and Nashville line. Late one dark and stormy night, an elderly station attendant became concerned that the torrential downpour might have eroded the gravel fill underneath a section of the tracks, posing a real danger for a freight train that was scheduled to pass through Chapel Hill at any minute. Donning his rain slicker, the trainman grabbed a lantern and proceeded down the slippery, sloping rail bed, keeping an eye out for sagging rails. When the oncoming freight train came into view, the signalman intended to flag it down by waving his lantern. However, the only life that was lost that night was his. The next morning, a railroad crew found the man's headless torso. No one knows for certain what happened. Some people believe that the man lost his footing on the wet rocks and hit his head on the rails, knocking himself unconscious. Others speculate that the signalman was standing between the rails waving his arms when his lantern suddenly went out. The coroner stated in his report that the signalman's head had been cut off by the steel wheels of the locomotive. His head was never found.

For more than a century, Chapel Hill has been known as the home of the ghost light. Witnesses claim that if someone stands between the rails facing north, a glowing ball appears out of nowhere. Suddenly the ghost light hurtles down the tracks directly toward the person standing on them. Some locals have reported that the ball of light appears to bounce around as it heads down the tracks. As a rule, the ghost light vanishes in just a few seconds. Sometimes months pass without a single sighting. In her book *13 Tennessee Ghosts and Jeffrey*, Kathryn Tucker Windham tells the story of a young man named Jackie Gentry who ventured down the L & N tracks one night with his uncle and a friend in hopes of seeing the light. The trio was just about to give up when Jackie spotted the ghost light bobbing up and down over the tracks about a hundred yards away. The boy quickly positioned himself in the middle of the tracks to get a better view. Without warning, the ghost light swooped down the tracks right toward Jackie. Before he could move a muscle, the light passed through his body and continued flying down the tracks until it disappeared from view. Jackie later recalled hearing a loud thud and feeling a sudden chill as the ghost light penetrated his body.

Not everyone accepts the folklore explanation for the ghost light of Chapel Hill. Scientists say that ghost lights could be caused by geological anomalies such as underground pools of liquid, subatomic particles, methane gas, or reflections from nearby towns. Many residents of Chapel Hill believe, however, that history might provide an answer to the mystery. Although there is no contemporary account of a trainman who was decapitated on the L & N line around Chapel Hill, local newspapers report that a man named Skip Adgent was struck and killed by a train in the area where the ghost light is seen. No one seems in a hurry to come up with a definitive explanation for the phenomenon, though. As long as the ghost light remains a mystery, light seekers will continue traveling to Chapel Hill.

Carter House Specters

The Battle of Franklin is also known as the "Gettysburg of the West" because of the devastating effect it had on the Confederacy's ability to win the Civil War. On November 18, 1864, General John Bell Hood's Confederate infantry joined forces with Nathan Bedford Forrest's cavalry in Tennessee. Hood had hoped that by doing so, he would be able to prevent Union general John Schofield from taking Nashville. At Spring Hill, less than thirty miles from Nashville, Hood flanked Schofield in an effort to cut him off. While Hood's troops slept, however, Schofield's army slipped away into the darkness and pushed on toward Nashville.

On November 30, Schofield was forced to stop his advance at Franklin because the bridge over the river was burned. While his engineers began work on a new bridge, the Federals took positions just south of town. At 2 P.M., Hood's army appeared on the rim of the hills south of Franklin. An hour later, Hood ordered an attack on the Union forces, which were entrenched in a huge semicircle. Fifteen brigades of Confederate troops swept forward like a tidal wave. The Federal line faltered at first from the relentless onslaught but eventually stiffened. Hood launched at least thirteen assaults against the Federal earthworks, but to no avail. At 9 P.M., Hood ordered an end to the slaughter. The Confederates lost 6,261 men and the Union 2,326 on what was one of the smallest battlefields of the Civil War. The home of one of the families who found themselves embroiled in the conflict still bears the physical—and apparently psychic—scars of the battle.

Fountain Branch Carter built his home in 1830 on what was then a gentle, rolling field. At the time of the Civil War, Fountain Branch was an elderly widower. Just before the battle, Union general James Dolson Cox took over the Carter House as a command post. On November 30, during the heat of the battle, Union general Emerson Opdycke's troops made a stand at the Carter House and proceeded to drive the Confederates back.

During the fierce fighting that ensued in and around the Carter House, Fountain Branch's oldest son, Moscow Branch Carter, herded his family into the cellar. Huddling in the darkness, the twenty-two family members, neighbors, and servants could not see the battle, but they could hear the sounds of men screaming, bullets thwacking against the boards, and even a cannonball crashing into the side of the house. They also saw a Union soldier scrambling for safety inside the house.

After the fighting ceased, a makeshift hospital for wounded Confederate soldiers was set up in the parlor of the Carter House. Late that night, Moscow crept out of the cellar. Picking up a lantern, he made his way through the battlefield, looking for his brother Tod, who had served on Confederate general T. B. Smith's staff. Smith arrived at the Carter House shortly after Moscow left and then joined the search. After probing among the dead and dying for what seemed an eternity, Moscow and General Smith found Tod lying wounded about a hundred yards away from the house. They carried him inside and placed him in a first-floor bedroom. His sisters tended to him for two days, until he finally died in the same room in which he was born.

The Carter House was purchased by the state of Tennessee in 1951. The registered National Historic Landmark now sits on eight acres and serves as a nonprofit museum and interpretive center for the Battle of Franklin. Visitors marvel at the more than one thousand bullet holes that are still visible to this day. They also enjoy hearing the ghost stories, which staff members will relate in private.

For years, poltergeistlike activity has been observed in the Carter House. Staff and visitors have heard disembodied voices, seemingly coming from nowhere. Some visitors have heard a woman's voice calling their names. Objects that were left in one room at night turn up in another room when the Carter House is reopened the next morning. Once during a tour, a young man pointed out to the tour guide that a statue behind her was jumping up and down. Staff members who have been left alone in the house have felt someone tugging at their sleeves. The culprit may be the spirit of Tod's little sister Annie, who has been seen running through an upstairs hall and down the stairs. She is also said to rearrange knickknacks, slam doors, and leave drawers open.

Tod's ghost has been observed as well in the Carter House. Several witnesses have seen the apparition of a young man sitting on the edge of the bed in which Tod died. His spirit always vanishes after materializing for a few seconds. The most dramatic sighting of Tod Carter was reported by a woman who served as a Carter House tour guide before becoming director. One evening, she was getting ready to close up when a young man walked in the front door, asking for a tour. Dressed in brown woolen pants with suspenders and a brown shirt, he had the look of someone from another time. As she related the history of the house and its former occupants, he corrected her when she used the wrong name or date. His know-it-all attitude angered her, but she concealed it as best she could.

When they had completed the tour of the lower floor, the tour guide was about to take him down into the cellar when he said, "We can't go down there." She turned around to tell him it would be all right, and he disappeared. Thinking that she had seen the young man before, she began looking through the photographs of the Carter family. She stopped when she came to a period photograph of Tod Carter: He was the young man who had taken a tour of his former residence. Like most good tour guides, she was receptive to learning anything new that could be added to her tours, especially if the information came from one of the former occupants.

The Phantoms of Carnton Plantation

Carnton Mansion in Franklin was built in 1826 by Randal McGavock, a former mayor of Nashville. After his death in 1843, Randal's son John inherited the plantation. Five years later, John married Carrie Elizabeth Winder. She gave birth to five children, only two of whom were still alive in 1862.

Life at Carnton was tranquil before the Civil War. Dignitaries such as Sam Houston and Presidents Andrew Jackson and James K. Polk were frequent guests at the elegant mansion. Then on November 30, 1864, Carnton was indirectly involved in one of the bloodiest clashes of the entire Civil War, the Battle of Franklin. On this date, Confederate general John Bell Hood attempted to destroy General John Schofield's Union forces before they could converge on Nashville. By the end of the five-hour battle, more than eighty-five hundred troops lay dead or wounded; more than six thousand of those soldiers were Confederates. Carnton, which was on the edge of the two-mile-long by one-and-a-half-mile-wide battlefield, was converted into the largest field hospital. Hundreds of wounded and dying Confederate soldiers received medical care inside the mansion from army surgeons and Carrie McGavock, who ordered the servants to roll up all of the carpets and tend to the wounded soldiers. She also fed her patients and tore up strips of cloth to serve as bandages.

More than two hundred men were treated at a time inside the house. The demand for hospital space was so great that many soldiers were treated in the yard. Doctors operated in the parlor; the dead were piled up on the back porch like cordwood. On the morning of December 1, the bodies of four Confederate generals killed during the battle—Patrick Cleburne, Hiram Granbury, John Adams, and Otho Strahl—were laid out on the back porch. So many amputations were performed inside the mansion that bloodstains can still be found on the wooden floors. In one of the upper bedrooms, a bloodstained circle marks the spot where a bloody bucket was placed during operations. But if the tales told by visitors and staff can be believed, blood is not the only remnant of the wounded soldiers that can still be found at Carnton Plantation.

One of the most haunted sites on Carnton Plantation is the cemetery. In 1866, John McGavock had the soldiers who had been hastily buried near the Carter House exhumed and reinterred on two acres of land adjacent to his family cemetery. Carrie recorded the names and additional information that was found on the bodies. Nearly fifteen hundred soldiers are buried there, making it the largest privately owned military cemetery in the entire nation. Some people have seen a spectral soldier standing guard inside the burial ground. Sometimes he follows visitors around until they leave the cemetery. Residents, visitors, and staff at Carnton Plantation also have seen the ghost of a little girl, thought to be the spirit of one of Carrie's three children who died, romping around the tombstones and running her hand along the fence. On some nights, the only evidence that the child's ghost is present is the distinctive sound that her hand makes against the fence.

Carrie Elizabeth's ghost has been seen as well. One day in the early 2000s, a tour guide named Margie was giving the last tour of the night. Meanwhile, Margie's eighteen-year-old daughter was in the gift shop. Toward the end of the tour, Margie was standing out in the cemetery, talking to a group of schoolchildren. Her daughter had left the gift shop and was sitting on the porch when she heard what she described as the shuffling of feet inside the house on the second floor. When the girl stepped outside and looked up, she saw a dark-haired woman wearing an old-fashioned white dress. The apparition's attention seemed to be fixed on the group standing in the cemetery. Suddenly the ghost faded into the night. Margie was just finishing up her tour when her daughter came running across the field yelling, "Mommy! Mommy!" Needless to say, the girl's story of her encounter certainly livened up the tour.

The most commonly seen spirit at Carnton Plantation is the ghost of a soldier who likes to walk through the house and across the back porch. He has also been observed marching around the perimeter of the yard. He is distinguished from the other ghosts on the plantation by the sound of his heavy boots. Author Christopher Coleman speculates that this male apparition could be the ghost of General Patrick Cleburne, who was supposedly seen standing on the veranda by a security guard one night during the Heritage Ball, a fund-raiser for Carnton Mansion. In the circle of light cast by his flashlight, the security guard could tell that he was an older man wearing a long, gray coat.

A number of other paranormal phenomena have also been experienced by staff and visitors. Several years ago, a Civil War reenactor took a photograph of the back of the mansion when no one was inside. When he examined the picture, he was surprised to see the face of a little girl staring out of one of the second-floor windows. A tour guide who looked at the picture said that it resembled Mary Elizabeth, a little girl who had died in the house. A couple years later, a woman told a tour guide that she detected a strange smell in the house. The tour guide asked her, "Was it perfume?" and the woman said no. The guide then suggested, "Was it blood?" and the woman became very serious and did not say anything.

In 1981, a twelve-year-old girl whose grandmother had just been made director of Carnton Mansion walked into the modernized kitchen alone, to find a slender African American woman standing with her back to her. The woman was wearing a floor-length skirt, a light-colored blouse, and a bandanna on her head. When the woman turned around, the girl could see right through her. The child shrieked and ran back to the foyer, where her grandmother and father were talking. They told the frightened girl that she had encountered the "kitchen ghost," believed to be the spirit of a slave who had been murdered by her jealous husband in the smokehouse in the late 1830s.

In 2006, my wife, Marilyn, and I were in a second-floor bedroom of Carnton Mansion by ourselves, when we heard a tapping sound on a pane of glass in one of the doors that opened to the veranda. We stared out onto the porch but could see no one. When we told the tour guide what we had heard, she said that this was the room General Nathan Bedford Forrest had stayed in when he visited the mansion. Carrie wrote in a letter that he entered the house, climbed the stairs, walked into this room, and went through the door onto the veranda. When he saw the Union soldiers approaching the battlefield, Forrest left the house without saying a word. The tour guide wondered whether his very brief stay in this room had left a psychic imprint of some sort.

Rookie tour guides at Carnton Mansion are told from the outset that staff members who are disrespectful to the spirits in the house are the ones who get picked on. One day, a new tour guide was downstairs when she heard some people upstairs talking about the ghosts in the house. It occurred to her that she could play on the fears of the tourists, so she walked over to the piano and played a couple notes. Just a few seconds later, several children ran downstairs, screaming. The tour guide told them, "I got you!" and then assured them that there were no ghosts in Carnton Mansion.

Later, as she was getting ready to lock up after the last tour, she began checking the windows and doors on the first floor to make sure they were locked. When she went over to the alarm, she heard footsteps walking down the hallway behind her. Paralyzed with fear, she refused to turn around to see what was standing behind her. All of a sudden she felt something push her out the door. The tour guide quit the next day.

The White Screamer

In *The Encyclopedia of Ghosts and Spirits*, Rosemary Guiley defines the word *banshee* as follows:

> a female death omen spirit of Ireland and Scotland that attaches itself to families . . . and manifests to herald an approaching death in the family. Traditionally, the banshee was believed to announce the imminent death of a loved one with a mournful wail. The Scotch-Irish immigrants who settled the southeastern United States brought these tales of banshees with them to their new home.

For some unknown reason, only a few banshee stories have become part of American folklore. One of the best-known, that of the White Screamer, is told in the town of White Bluff.

In the standard version of the story, a young man built his family a home in an isolated hollow near White Bluff. The first night the man and his family spent in their new home, they were awakened in the middle of the night by a bone-chilling scream. Every night, the family heard the high-pitched wail. After a few sleepless nights, the man's wife and children could take no more. They persuaded him to try to hunt down the screamer, whatever it was, and kill it. Late one evening, the man picked up his rifle and, accompanied by his faithful dogs, walked out the front door of the cabin.

He had not gone very far into the woods before the screaming began. Immediately the baying hounds took off in the direction of the sound. Thinking that he was about to bring his family's suffering to an end, the man ran after his dogs. Suddenly the screaming was replaced by the unmistakable sound of whimpering. Within just a few seconds of taking up the chase, the dogs returned with their tails between their legs.

Most men would have followed the dogs home, but the man was determined to bring peace to his family. He decided to climb up a steep incline to get a better view of the surrounding countryside. The man had just reached the top of the hill when he heard screaming. This time, though, the screams were human, and they were coming from his cabin. Fearing for his family's safety, the man ran all the way back home. After what seemed an eternity, he reached his cabin. The eerie stillness made his heart beat even faster. Panting heavily, he threw open the door. The sight that greeted his eyes was replayed in nightmares for the remainder of his life. There on the bloody floor lay the mangled bodies of his wife and children.

Generations of residents of White Bluff have heard the tragic tale of the victims of the White Screamer. People say that the stone foundations of the old cabin can still be seen out in the woods. Those who report having actually seen the White Screamer describe it as a translucent female ghost. Burned patches of grass bear witness to the phantom's presence. To this day, the wailing of the wind or the howling of dogs late at night still raises goose bumps in White Bluff.

The Ghosts of Stones River

After Christmas in 1862, Union major general William S. Rosecrans moved the Army of the Cumberland south from Nashville toward Murfreesboro. His objective was to drive Confederate general Braxton Bragg's Army of Tennessee out of the state. Bragg's army had been encamped at Murfreesboro for a month. The Union force numbered forty-four thousand men, while the Confederates had thirty-eight thousand. When Rosecrans failed to attack on December 30, Bragg decided to move against the Union right flank at dawn, catching the Federals completely by surprise. Federal ammunition trains were captured by the Confederate cavalry, and as a result, Rosecrans's soldiers were completely out of bullets by 11 A.M. Many troops were ordered to hold their ground with bayonets and, if need be, their rifle butts.

At a section of the battlefield now known as the Slaughter Pen, General Phil Sheridan fought a chaotic battle in the woods to give Rosecrans time to organize a proper defense. While neighboring units to Sheridan's right collapsed, his brigades of men from Illinois and Missouri stood strong, even after the fight had come down to hand-to-hand combat with bayonets. Eventually Sheridan found himself hemmed in on three sides. Still, his men were able to withstand three successive Confederate assaults before they were forced to retreat. Thanks to the sacrifices made by Sheridan's troops, Rosecrans was able to re-form his lines by 4 P.M., but he was unable to mount an attack. On the morning of New Year's Day 1863, Bragg was surprised to find that the Union Army had not pulled back to Nashville. Late in the afternoon, the Confederates charged but were repulsed by Union artillery. After Bragg learned from captured documents that Union reinforcements had arrived, he retreated thirty-six miles to the south. The Union had lost thirteen thousand men, and the Confederates nearly twelve thousand. Some say that the psychic residue from these horrific casualties still remains at Stones River National Battlefield and Cemetary.

Not surprisingly, the most haunted area in the military park is Stop No. 4 on the battlefield driving tour, the Slaughter Pen. A strange stillness has been known to descend here on days when wildlife is active in other parts of the battlefield. Park rangers passing through the area at night after closing hours have heard footsteps walking behind them. One ranger says that as a rule, the Slaughter Pen is 10 or 20 degrees colder than the rest of the park. Some reenactors camping at the Slaughter Pen claim that a mysterious soldier occasionally shows up when the men are discussing battle strategy. He is said to sit close to the flames, hunched over, as if he is trying to keep warm. He has also been seen standing next to a tree or sitting on a stone outcropping. The spectral soldier usually dematerializes when someone walks up to him and attempts to communicate.

The wife of a park ranger encountered a female revenant at the spot. One day, while she was walking through the Slaughter Pen, she had a vision of a woman running across the field and screaming. Her curiosity aroused, she did some research and discovered that a black school had been set up near the Slaughter Pen after the Civil War. The school's white teacher was murdered.

A different entity has been known to materialize around Stop No 6. Troy Taylor, in *Spirits of the Civil War*, says that a park ranger named Jeffrey Leathers was asleep after reenacting the Battle of Stones River. He woke up in the middle of the night to get a drink of water at the administration building when he detected what appeared to be a man hiding in the bushes just off the path. Thinking that the man was a fellow reenactor who was trying to frighten him, Jeffrey ordered him to come out of the bushes. The man emerged from his hiding place with his hands raised, as if he were surrendering, and walked toward Jeffrey. When the man got a little too close for comfort, Jeffrey ordered him to stop, but the strange man continued walking in Jeffrey's direction. Still in character, Jeffrey raised his rifle, and as he did so, the man fell to the ground and disappeared. The next day, Jeffrey combed the area for footprints but found only his own.

It is not surprising that a national park with areas called the Slaughter Pen and Hell's Half Acre is haunted. What is surprising, though, is that more people have not experienced the paranormal there. One wonders how many ghostly soldiers, like the male ghost at the Slaughter Pen, may have successfully blended in with the thousands of reenactors who visit the park each year.

The Haunted Hermitage

The stately mansion that eventually became home to a president of the United States was originally a two-story log farmhouse. On July 5, 1804, Nathaniel Hays sold his log cabin and the adjoining farm to Andrew Jackson for $3,400. After workmen cleared the fields and wallpapered the interior of the farmhouse, Andrew and his wife Rachel moved to their plantation. Jackson had originally called it Rural Retreat, but for some unknown reason, he changed the name to the Hermitage.

Jackson's slaveholdings grew from nine in 1804 to forty-four in 1820. His thousand-acre plantation included a dairy, cotton gin and press, distillery, and slave cabins. Jackson's primary cash crop was cotton; most of the vegetables raised on the farm were used to feed Jackson's family and the slaves. Between 1819 and 1821, skilled carpenters and masons built a two-story Federal style brick mansion for Jackson and his family. After Jackson became president in 1829, his son Andrew Jackson Jr. took over the day-to-day operation of the plantation. In 1831, architect David Morrison added a front entrance portico, a small rear entrance portico, copper gutters, and flanking one-story wings. An elaborate limestone tomb with a copper dome was built in 1831-32 for Rachel, who had died in 1828.

After Jackson left the U.S. presidency in 1837, he retired to the Hermitage, where he lived until his death on June 8, 1845. His body was placed in a tomb next to Rachel's. Andrew Jackson Jr. took care of the daily operations of the plantation until 1856, when he sold five hundred acres, including the Hermitage, to the state of Tennessee. He and his family remained at the Hermitage until 1858, when he moved to a cotton plantation in Mississippi. He returned to the Hermitage in 1860 and was still living there when he died in 1865.

Within a few years, the Hermitage fell into disrepair. In 1888, plans were under way to convert the Hermitage into a Confederate Soldiers' Home. Then in April 1889, the Ladies' Hermitage Association (LHA) was chartered. The LHA persuaded the legislature to turn the Hermitage over to them; a Confederate Soldiers' Home would be built elsewhere on the plantation. The LHA was granted control over the twenty-five-acre core section of the Hermitage farm. In the 1950s and 1960s, the LHA enlarged the size of the farm by purchasing adjoining lands. Today 1,120 acres are under the control of the LHA, including Andrew Jackson's original 1,050-acre tract. The ladies of the LHA still talk about that time in 1893 when President Jackson returned to the Hermitage.

In *Strange Tales of the Dark and Bloody Ground*, Christopher Coleman says that in July 1893, two members of the Ladies Hermitage Association, Mary Dorris and Mary Baxter, rode up to the front steps of the Hermitage with the intention of staying there until a caretaker could be found in order to protect the old mansion from vandals. They were met at the door by Andrew Jackson's former valet, who was deaf and nearly blind, and the housekeeper, a young black woman from a nearby farm. The ladies immediately began locking all the doors and windows in the house. After dinner, they sat on the front porch to take in the cool evening air. As the sun went down, the distinctive cry of a screech owl sent shivers up their spines.

When darkness fell, the ladies placed a mattress on the floor of the front parlor and fell asleep. They were awakened after several hours by the clanging sound of pots and pans in the kitchen. A few minutes later, they heard what sounded like plates and dishes being piled on the floor. From the porch came the clanking of chains. The ladies' terror escalated when they heard the unmistakable sound of a horse being ridden up and down the upstairs hallways. Once their initial shock subsided, one of the ladies turned on the kerosene lamp that they had brought along. At that instant, the commotion abruptly ceased.

The next morning, the ladies combed the entire house, looking for the source of the eerie sounds, but they found nothing in any of the closets or cabinets that could have caused the noises. That night, they prepared once again to sleep on their mattress, but this time they kept the kerosene lamp turned on. After midnight, the ladies heard the same sounds as the night before: the throwing of pots and pans, the stacking of dishes, the clanking of chains, and the pounding hoofbeats of a horse galloping through the upstairs hallways.

Night after night, the bizarre noises continued to disturb the sleep of the vigilant ladies. The women never really became accustomed to the sounds, but they were no longer paralyzed with fear as they had been the first time they heard the clamor. Understandably, they were greatly relieved when a full-time caretaker was finally hired. It was years before they were able to tell anyone about their encounter with the entity they believed was the spirit of Andrew Jackson. Paranormal investigators speculate that Jackson's spirit might have been awakened by the ongoing restoration of the old house.

Dutiful Daughters

Capitol Records Nashville is home to one of the most popular labels in country music. Artists such as Trace Adkins, Merle Haggard, Kenny Rogers, Keith Urban, and Eric Church have all recorded for Capitol. The company also produces and distributes comedy albums by such comedians as Tim Wilson and Roy D. Mercer. If the stories can be believed, however, the Old Capitol Records Building at 1111 16th Avenue, in the heart of Music Row, has a couple of "star attractions" who never want to leave.

The building was constructed on a site that was once the property of a grain merchant named Jacob Schnell. Around 1900, Schnell built a magnificent home where he anticipated that he, his wife, and their two daughters, Lena and Bertha, would entertain the most elite members of society. He hoped to help his family gain admittance into high society by throwing a grand ball. To Schnell's dismay, however, none of the invited guests showed up. Schnell vented his frustration and anger by moving back to his apartment over his feed and grain store. He ordered his daughters to remain in the mansion and do nothing to maintain it. Schnell planned to take his revenge on society by allowing his house to become an eyesore.

Over the years, both the house and the mental condition of Lena and Bertha began to deteriorate. In *Strange Tales of the Dark and Bloody Ground*, Christopher Coleman reports that after Lena died, Bertha was so convinced that her sister was still alive that she did not notify authorities. Lena's corpse remained in the house until neighbors alerted the Health Department. Following Bertha's death, the once imposing mansion was razed.

Paranormal activity began not long after the Old Capitol Records Building was opened for business. Several mornings, employees discovered unrolled reams of toilet paper on the floor. On one occasion, they found it impossible to heat the storage room. Before long, employees began hearing footsteps in a deserted hallway. Doors that they remembered unlocking seemed to lock themselves a few minutes later, and several employees observed doors opening and closing on their own. The ventilation system turned off and on by itself. Objects that were left in one location were found in an entirely different place the next day. Frequently employees have answered a call from an inside phone, only to find that no one is on the line.

William C. Uchtman says in *Volunteer Ghosts* that one day, an employee placed a package of Oreo cookies in the kitchen just before a meeting began. After the meeting ended, she returned to the kitchen and was shocked to find that all of the cookies in the package had been crushed. On another occasion, a male employee tried four times to open a door. Exasperated, he exclaimed, "Quit it Bertha!" He inserted his key in the lock, and the door opened freely. So far, the entity has been seen to materialize only once. The witness said that it appeared in front of her desk as a spiral of mist or smoke. No one had been smoking in the building at the time.

The eleven-story office building that now houses Capitol Records is truly a colorless substitute for the fine home that once stood there. Many believe that Lena and Bertha Schnell still dutifully reside at the site in compliance with their father's demand that they remain there. Or perhaps the disturbances that occur at the Old Capitol Records Building on a regular basis are a sign that Jacob is still angry at the city that rejected him and his family.

Restless Nights at Falcon Rest

Clay Faulkner is remembered today as one of Tennessee's great nineteenth-century entrepreneurs. In 1873, he opened Mountain City Woolen Mills. After mineral springs were discovered on the grounds, Faulkner converted the woolen mills into Faulkner Springs Hotel health resort. He also supervised the construction of the Great Falls Cotton Mill and the McMinnville Methodist Church, both at Rock Island.

In 1896, he built Falcon Rest—the solid brick, ten-thousand-square-foot mansion that has been called "Tennessee's Biltmore"—for his wife. Faulkner's state-of-the-art home in McMinnville featured indoor plumbing, central heat, and electric lights. In the 1940s, Falcon Rest was converted into a hospital and nursing home. Following additions made to the house in the mid-1950s, Dr. J. P. Dietrich renamed it the Faulkner Springs Hospital. When the hospital closed in 1968, Dr. Dietrich removed the woodwork so that he could get to the brick and tear down the house, but he was unsuccessful.

For almost two decades, the dilapidated old mansion stood vacant. Then in 1989, George and Charlien McGlothin purchased the property and embarked on a four-year restoration project. In 1993, the couple renamed Clay Faulkner's dream house Falcon Manor and reopened it as a bed-and-breakfast, and they celebrated the building's 110th anniversary in April 2006 by changing its name back to Falcon Rest. The splendor of the Victorian Age is evident in the inn's bountiful antiques—and, some say, in occasional appearances of its original occupants.

Paranormal activity was reported in Falcon Rest not long after Clay Faulkner died in 1916. Faulkner's relatives reported hearing disembodied footsteps on the stairs. The pungent aroma of Faulkner's cigar smoke wafted through unoccupied rooms. An object placed in a particular room often found its way somehow to a completely different location the next morning. Electric lights switched on and off by themselves.

After the old mansion received its new incarnation as a bed-and-breakfast in 1993, members of the staff began having bizarre experiences almost immediately. One Christmas season, a young man who was decorating a tree all by himself asked the lady in the visitors center if anyone had entered the building in the past few minutes. When she said no, he explained that he had become so filled with the Christmas spirit while hanging the ornaments that he started whistling "It Came upon a Midnight Clear." As soon as he stopped whistling, the young man distinctly heard spectral whistling that continued for a few seconds and then moved down the stairs. At Falcon Rest, the phrase "Christmas spirit" takes on an entirely different meaning.

In 2003, a tour guide was talking in one of the bedrooms when a young woman reported seeing the apparition of a lady walking through the front door. The guide, Liz, assured her that Falcon Rest had no reenactors but it did have "inhabitants." Suddenly, the entire house was rocked by what seemed to be an explosion. Fearing what she would find, Liz went ahead with the tour. Surprisingly, nothing in the house seemed to have been broken or harmed in any way. During the next tour, however, Liz discovered that the antique mirror that usually hung over the dining-room buffet was now on the floor. When she examined the ornate mirror, she was shocked to find that it was in perfect condition. Because the mirror had almost fallen on two previous occasions, George McGlothin decided to leave it where the ghosts had dropped it.

Upon reflection, Liz concluded that the ghost had caused the racket to verify her statement regarding the inhabitants of the house. Several years ago, a movie director staying at the bed-and-breakfast confirmed Liz's suspicion that the house is haunted. "I feel a real presence here, but it is friendly, curious, and just wants to be known," he said.

Today guests staying at the bed-and-breakfast, which its owners bill as "the Victorian mansion where history is fun," are offered entertainment in addition to good food and soft beds. Building on the success of his interactive mystery play and meal, "Murder at the Mansion," George has now produced a ghost show titled "Ghosts at the Mansion." Staff at the bed-and-breakfast serve as the "host ghosts." The roles of actual people are played by guests, who are encouraged to ad-lib their lines. The only qualification, George says, is that the guests take the roles of people who were interesting and are now dead. Maybe some day, old Clay Faulkner will make a cameo appearance and add a little verisimilitude to the play that he inspired.

Strange Occurrences at the Walking Horse Hotel

The little town of Wartrace derived its name from a trail used by Native Americans. It became known as Wartrace Depot after the Nashville and Chattanooga Railroad was completed through eastern Bedford County in 1851. For more than fifty years, a number of hotels were constructed to accommodate the influx of visitors to the town. One of the best known of these old inns, the Walking Horse Hotel, was built in 1917 by Jesse and Nora Overall. In the 1930s, Wartrace acquired a reputation not only as a major railroad town, but also as the walking horse capital of the world. Many residents of Wartrace believe that the Walking Horse Hotel has long been haunted by the ghost of a former owner of the old inn.

In the 1930s, Floyd Carothers was a horse trainer who, along with Henry Davis, purchased a promising walking horse named Strolling Jim. Carothers boarded the horse in the old stables behind the hotel he had owned since 1933, the Walking Horse Hotel. Thanks to Carothers's skills as a trainer and Strolling Jim's natural ability, the horse won blue ribbons in every competition he entered. The true test came in 1939, when Strolling Jim became the first horse to be crowned world champion walking horse in Shelbyville. That same year, Floyd Carothers sold Strolling Jim, and the horse continued to win awards. In 1957, after being put to pasture, Strolling Jim died. Floyd's wife, Olive, buried the horse behind the hotel, which she continued to run after her husband died in 1944.

The fact that Floyd Carothers was also buried near the Walking Horse Hotel might have something to do with the paranormal activity that has been reported there over the years. George Wright, who was manager of the hotel from 1980 to 1993, said that in the early 1980s, he had a photograph taken of himself and a guest sitting at the dining-room table. George had intended to use the picture in a brochure for the hotel. He was unable to use the photograph, however, because after it was developed, it clearly showed two shimmering figures standing behind George and his guest.

George Wright experienced the protective side of Floyd in 1991. In *Haunted Hotels*, Robin Mead says that for several days in late June of that year, the hotel's security cameras were malfunctioning. On

July 1, when George was particularly busy, a number of unexplained disturbances at the hotel were making things even more hectic. Suddenly he felt compelled to go to the stalls in the back of the hotel, where a prize mare was starting to foal. He could tell immediately that the mare was having a difficult time, so he contacted a veterinarian, who delivered the colt at 1:30 the next morning.

In 1995, the Walking Horse Hotel was bought by John and Bea Garland. The new owners changed the name to Hotel Overall in honor of the original owners. They also completely renovated the old building, installing central heat and air-conditioning and filling the hotel with period antiques. In *Strange Tales of the Dark and Bloody Ground*, Christopher Coleman says that one New Year's Eve, several local residents rented the hotel for a night of alcohol- and drug-free celebrating. Suddenly at midnight, the guests witnessed the ghost of Strolling Jim prancing around his grave behind the hotel. Afterward, all of the witnesses swore that alcohol was not a factor in the sighting of the spectral champion.

According to the website *Strangeusa.com*, a tragedy that happened in the 1970s might also be responsible for some of the bizarre occurrences. Supposedly a Vietnam veteran who had been suffering from flashbacks went on a bloody rampage one night, shooting and stabbing four other guests in the hotel. For several years afterward, guests reported hearing disembodied voices, gunshots, and footsteps running up and down the hallways at night. They also reported feeling as if they were being watched in Room 11.

After closing down in the mid-2000s, the old hotel reopened in the fall of 2007 under its previous name, the Walking Horse Hotel. Tourists are attracted to the four-star hotel's gift shops and its quaint charm, enhanced by such period touches as claw-foot bathtubs. Paranormal activity at the hotel dropped off sharply after the death of Olive Carothers in 1991, so guests today are likely to spend a peaceful night at the Walking Horse.

The Unquiet Spirit of Meriwether Lewis

The names of Meriwether Lewis and William Clark have become synonymous with Western exploration and expansion. Lewis had served six years in the Frontier Army when President Thomas Jefferson appointed him to be his personal secretary in 1801. Lewis, who had been a childhood friend of Jefferson's, discussed the exploration of a westward route to the Pacific coast. After the signing of the Louisiana Purchase on April 30, 1803, Meriwether Lewis chose his former superior officer, Captain William Clark, to assist him on his journey out west. Their mission was to draw maps; collect plant, animal, and mineral specimens; clear the way for commerce; and establish friendly relations with the various Indian tribes. After returning safely to St. Louis in September 1806, Lewis began a downward spiral from which he never recovered. Lewis's ignominious death on the Natchez Trace remains one of the greatest tragedies—and mysteries—in American history.

In a show of gratitude for the great service Lewis had performed for the nation, President Jefferson appointed him governor of the Louisiana Territory. Before long, though, Lewis's personal problems began to affect his administration. He sank deeply into debt after paying for medicine he had promised the Indians. He began drinking heavily after losing money in bad land investments and quarreled with people such as Frederick Bates, a subordinate whom Lewis turned into a lifelong enemy after humiliating him in public. Fearing that his enemies, such as Bates, were spreading rumors that he was planning to separate the Louisiana Territory from the United States, Lewis decided to travel to Washington, D.C., and defend himself against these false charges.

In September 1809, Lewis and a small party of men caught a riverboat for Memphis. They had intended to eventually travel down to New Orleans and then make their way to Washington from there. While going down the river, Lewis's drinking increased his dark mood to the point that he tried to commit suicide twice. Rumors that British ships were patrolling the Gulf of Mexico compelled him to travel to Washington by land instead. Although he was plagued with headaches and a raging fever, Lewis and his men set out in early October on the Natchez Trace, the primary overland route at that time.

On October 9, Lewis and his party sought refuge from a torrential downpour at Grinder's Inn near Hohenwald, which was seventy-two miles from Nashville. Mrs. Grinder informed Lewis that her husband was off hunting, and she was alone in the cabin except for her children and a servant. After leading him to his room, she offered to make a bed for Lewis, but he preferred to make a pallet of bearskins and a buffalo robe. Before retiring for the night, Lewis smoked a pipe and complained to her about his enemies in Washington, while pacing back and forth on the front lawn. When everyone in the house had retired for the night, Lewis continued to walk back and forth and talk to himself in his room.

Suddenly, in the middle of the night, Mrs. Grinder heard a gunshot and someone saying, "Oh, Lord!" Another gunshot immediately followed. Not long thereafter, she heard Lewis's voice at her door, pleading with her to give him some water and heal his wounds. Fearing for her safety and that of her children, she refused to open the door. She then heard the sound of Lewis half crawling, half walking to the kitchen, where he attempted to pour himself some water. Two hours later, Lewis's men, who had been sleeping in the barn, found their leader lying in his room on a bloodsoaked buffalo robe. He had been shot in the side and forehead and had also been slashed several times by a knife. In a weak, trembling voice, Lewis said, "I am no coward. But I am strong, so hard to die." He passed away just as dawn was breaking. Lewis was buried not far from the inn.

An investigation into Lewis's death began soon after the news reached Washington. The authorities who questioned Mrs. Grinder wondered why she had waited so long to check in on Lewis after he cried for help. They could not understand why those in Lewis's party did not hear the gunshots. They also questioned her statement that after the gunshots rang out through the inn, she found Lewis in his room "cutting himself from hand to foot with a razor." The investigators wondered how Lewis could have shot himself in the chest with a single-shot black powder pistol, reloaded it, shot himself in the head, and then mutilated himself with a razor while crying for help. In addition, they assumed that a man who was as familiar with firearms as Lewis would have done a much better job of killing himself. A year later, John Grinder was accused of murdering his famous guest, but the charges were eventually dismissed. Even though Lewis's supporters staunchly refused to believe that he had killed himself, suicide became the official cause of death.

Not long after Lewis's death, Grinder's Inn gained a local reputation as a haunted house. It was said that doors opened and closed themselves after midnight. Some guests at the inn reported seeing a male apparition standing by the well. When anyone walked up and tried to talk to him, the figure always vanished. Travelers riding past Lewis's grave said they could see a strange light near the burial site. People who were said to be extremely sensitive to the paranormal reported walking up to the front door of Grinder's Inn and being overcome with such a strong feeling of dread that they could not enter the cabin. Some passersby said they could hear a voice pleading for help coming from Lewis's grave.

In the 1920s, Lewis's remains were exhumed, and markings on his bones were compared with descriptions of the wounds in the investigators' reports filed in 1810. Once it was determined that the remains really did belong to Lewis, his grave was cemented over. Today only the stone foundation of Grinder's cabin remains. A replica of the original cabin has been built nearby, along with a circular granite column rising from a square base of native rock. Officials at Meriwether Lewis Park discourage people familiar with the old ghost stories from investigating the site, especially around Halloween. Visitors are intrigued by rumors that a spectral presence still hovers around the site. Locals also say that sometimes one can hear a voice whispering, "It is so hard to die," in the rustling trees. Until the mystery surrounding Lewis's death is finally solved, the explorer's restless spirit likely will continue to haunt the site of Grinder's Inn.

The Wraiths of Ryman Auditorium

The Ryman Auditorium has achieved fame as the home of the Grand Ole Opry, but it was originally built as a house of worship. On May 10, 1885, a steamboat captain named Thomas Green Ryman and a group of his rowdy friends decided to attend one of Reverend Samuel Porter Jones's weekly tent meetings. At the time, Ryman had earned a reputation as a drinker and a troublemaker on the Ohio, Cumberland, and Mississippi Rivers. On this fateful day in May, Ryman and his friends strolled into the tent revival with the intention of disrupting the proceedings.

Ironically, by the end of the meeting, Ryman had become a born-again Christian. Not only did he ban gambling and drinking on his steamboats, but he also set about to build a large religious center. Ryman's vision of a church where people of different faiths could come together and worship came to fruition in 1892 with the opening of the Union Gospel Tabernacle. The $2,700 building was large enough to seat 1,255 people. Before long, the Tabernacle became a venue for public meetings as well. In 1897, a huge balcony was added to accommodate a reunion of Confederate veterans. Because the veterans donated the money for the project, the balcony was named the Confederate Gallery in their honor.

After Thomas Green Ryman's death on December 23, 1904, Reverend Jones persuaded the members of the congregation to rename the Tabernacle the Ryman Auditorium. For the next four decades, the Ryman Auditorium served primarily as a theater. It hosted a variety of politicians, lecturers, performers, and entertainers, including Booker T. Washington, Teddy Roosevelt, Carrie A. Nation, John Philip Sousa, Charlie Chaplin, Douglas Fairbanks, Enrico Caruso, Sarah Bernhardt, Isadora Duncan, Rudolph Valentino, Will Rogers, Ethel Barrymore, Orson Welles, Helen Hayes, Doris Day, Eleanor Roosevelt, Katharine Hepburn, Bela Lugosi, Bob Hope, Harpo Marx, and Elvis Presley. On June 5, 1943, the WSM radio show *The Grand Ole Opry* began broadcasting from the Ryman Auditorium. For the next thirty years, some of the biggest stars in country-western music took the stage at the Ryman. In 1974, The Grand Ole Opry moved to its present home near the Gaylord Opryland Resort and Convention Center. According to legend, though, the Opry left behind the spirits of three people in the Ryman Auditorium.

One of these spirits is the ghost of Captain Ryman himself. In the years following his death, it is said that Ryman made it very clear when he did not approve of a performance held at his auditorium. The story goes that during a production of *Carmen* at the auditorium in the early 1900s, Ryman's ghost objected so strongly to the "adult" content of the opera that he began thrashing about. In fact, his ghost made so much commotion that patrons complained of being unable to hear the singing. This particular story is probably apocryphal, because *Carmen* was produced at the Union Gospel Tabernacle in 1901, three years before Ryman's death. First-hand accounts from witnesses indicate, however, that productions held in the theater after Ryman's death were interrupted by a very noisy, otherworldly presence.

Apparently Captain Ryman's ghost has been heard in the old theater as well. Once a skeptical production crew from New York decided to spend the night in the auditorium to see if the stories they had been told about Captain Ryman's ghost were true. Nothing out of the ordinary happened until midnight, when the members of the crew began hearing footsteps coming from the balcony. On close inspection, they noticed little specks of dust floating from the seams in the ceiling panels under the balcony every time they heard a footstep. The production crew returned to New York convinced that the Ryman Auditorium was indeed haunted.

A spirit identified only as the Gray Man is also said to haunt the Ryman. A number of people have reported seeing a man dressed in gray clothing sitting in the balcony after the auditorium has closed. As a rule, any janitors or security guards who climb the balcony stairs to question the man find no one there. When they return to the first floor, however, and glance back up at the balcony, the Gray Man has returned to his seat. Some people believe that the Gray Man is one of the Confederate veterans who tended to create a ruckus in the Confederate Gallery. The Gray Man has been sighted during rehearsals but never during actual performances.

The best-known ghost in the Ryman Auditorium is undoubtedly the spirit of country-western icon Hank Williams. One Saturday afternoon not long after Williams's death, Bill Anderson was sitting by himself in the auditorium, strumming one of Hank's favorite songs, when suddenly all the power in the entire building kicked off. The microphones, the lights, the amplifiers—everything went dead. Afterward, Anderson attributed the blackout to mechanical failure, although he suspected that the superstar might have been making his presence known that afternoon.

One witness actually claimed to have seen Hank's ghost in the Ryman Auditorium. In the early 1990s, when the theater was being renovated, a workman was accidentally locked in by himself after hours. He was walking through building when he confronted what he claimed was the misty likeness of Hank Williams.

It is said that every theater has its resident ghost. Often it is thought to be the spirit of a maintenance man who tumbled from a catwalk. The Ryman Auditorium differs from the run-of-the-mill theaters, however, in that two of its ghosts have achieved celebrity status.

Adelicia Acklen's Apparition

Belmont Mansion, built in the Italianate style at 1900 Belmont Boulevard in Nashville, was originally located on a lavish estate consisting of gardens, conservatories, a lake, a greenhouse, an aviary, and even a zoo! The 750 slaves who worked in the cotton fields and inside the house lived in a ninety-four-hundred-square-foot service area in the basement. The eleven-thousand-square-foot grand house was the summer home of Adelicia and Joseph Acklen, who owned an eighty-four-hundred-acre cotton plantation in Louisiana. Before marrying Joseph, Adelicia had been married to a wealthy man many years her senior named Isaac Franklin. She and Isaac had four children, all of whom died before the age of twelve. Adelicia and Isaac were married for only seven years when he died suddenly.

In 1849, Adelicia married Joseph Acklen. Construction on their dream villa, Belmont Mansion, was finally completed in 1850. For almost a decade, she and her husband hosted lavish parties that started after 11 P.M. and often lasted until dawn. Guests were served water with ice cubes, an extravagance reserved only for the rich. But wealth did not insulate Adelicia from tragedy. Adelicia's twin daughters died of scarlet fever. Her second husband, Joseph, was killed in the Civil War. In 1880, Adelicia started a college for women. After selling Belmont Mansion in 1887, Adelicia moved to Washington, D.C., where she died a few months later.

The endowment that Adelicia had left to the college allowed it to continue. In 1951, the Tennessee Baptist Convention began work on a co-ed version of Belmont College. The college became a teaching university in 1991. The centerpiece of the university is Belmont Mansion, which is now a historical museum. The old house stands as a monument to a strong, resilient woman who survived some of the cruelest blows that life can deal out. Some even claim that Adelicia has survived death itself.

It seems that Adelicia's ghost has been making frequent appearances at Belmont Mansion ever since her death in 1887. Museum staff and security guards claim to have seen her misty figure, dressed in an antebellum gown, walking in the building at night. She has also been observed staring out of one of the darkened upstairs windows. A young woman was walking around the corner of a hallway late one evening when she almost ran into the seemingly solid form of a woman dressed in a stylish gown from the mid-1800s. The young woman turned on her heels and ran out of the building as fast as she could. A security guard reported that another night, a woman wearing a hoop dress told him that the furniture was arranged incorrectly. The man still recalls the authoritative tone in the woman's voice.

Several theories have been offered to explain the return of Adelicia Acklen to her beautiful mansion. Some say that she continues to watch over the mansion, which was under her complete control after the death of Joseph. Others believe that she is drawn to the old house because it was the scene of some of the happiest and saddest times of her entire life. If Adelicia actually has returned from the dead, it is safe to speculate that she has done so for love, be it love of money, love of power, love for her children, or love for one of the grandest antebellum mansions in the entire state of Tennessee.

East Tennessee

EAST TENNESSEE IS A MOUNTAINOUS, LARGELY RURAL AREA THAT INCLUDES the Appalachian Plateau, the Appalachian Ridge and Valley Region, and the Blue Ridge Region. The plateau is famous for its V-shaped valleys. This is a mineral-rich area, producing thousands of tons of coal, petroleum, and natural gas every year.

The Appalachian Ridge and Valley Region extends westward from the Blue Ridge Region. It consists of narrow ridges and broad valleys in the eastern part of the area. This feature is called the Great Valley. More coal is mined in this area than in any other part of the state. The region's fertile farmland is surrounded by heavily forested ridges.

The Blue Ridge region along the eastern edge of Tennessee is the most mountainous part of the entire state. The average elevation of the region is 5,000 feet. Clingman's Dome, the highest point in Tennessee, is 6,643 feet high. This scenic area includes popular tourist spots such as Great Smoky Mountains National Park, Gatlinburg, and Pigeon Forge.

The Long Dog of Surgoinsville

In the first half of the nineteenth century, traveling through the mountainous regions of East Tennessee was fraught with danger. Pioneers had to contend with unpredictable weather, hostile Indians, and seemingly impassable trails. At that time, a new type of outlaw known as a "land pirate" made travel even more perilous. The most notorious of these scoundrels was John Murrell. Born in 1804, Murrell was the son of an itinerant preacher and the madam of a brothel, named Zilpah. At a very early age, Murrell's mother encouraged him to sneak into her bedroom while she was "occupying" her customers and steal their wallets. Murrell also received training in the art of thievery from a semiretired sea pirate named Harry Cranshaw.

While he was still a teenager, Murrell stole unprotected horses or slaves from their owners and resold them. His criminal career was put on hold for a short period after he was arrested for stealing a black mare from a widow. Following his guilty verdict, Murrell's thumb was branded with the letters "HT" for horse thief. He was also flogged and incarcerated. After Murrell was released from prison a year later, Cranshaw transformed the young thief into a murderous cutthroat and bushwhacker. In the 1820s, Murrell and Cranshaw ambushed travelers on lonely roads, shot them, robbed them, and then dumped their bodies into ponds, lakes, or rivers. The only victim Murrell and Cranshaw did not dispose of properly forms the basis of one of East Tennessee's most enduring ghost stories.

Some time in the late 1820s or early 1830s, a family of settlers who were making their way to Nashville were camping along the Old Sage Road a few miles outside of Surgoinsville. They were sleeping under the sheltering limbs of a large white oak tree atop a small hill when they were aroused from their sleep by John Murrell and Harry Cranshaw. The bandits' relentless threats and questioning eventually compelled the father to reveal the location of their valuables. Once Murrell and Cranshaw had found the family's possessions, the travelers' usefulness had come to an end. Every member of the family of settlers was murdered in cold blood, including the children.

The next order of business was to load the valuables and the bodies of the family members onto their wagon. Murrell and Cranshaw were headed down the road, looking for a body of water where they could dump the corpses, when they noticed that they were being followed by the family pet, a long, white dog with short legs. Murrell stopped the wagon and walked toward the animal with the intention of adopting it as his own. He knelt down to pet the dog, fully expecting her to succumb to his blue-eyed charm, just as so many of his human victims had. Instead, the dog growled and clamped down on Murrell's hand in a viselike grip. Screaming at the top of his lungs, Murrell jumped up and down, with the dog firmly attached to his hand. After several attempts, Cranshaw finally managed to wrap his hands around the dog's neck and choke her. Before long, the dog slipped into unconsciousness, enabling Murrell to open her jaws and drop her to the ground. Murrell's anger at having his gestures of friendship so violently rebuked, along with his fear of contracting rabies, drove him to strangle the little dog in his powerful hands. He then threw the heroic little canine into a roadside ditch.

In 1834, after years of larceny and murder, John Murrell was finally indicted, found guilty, and sentenced to ten years in prison. Because none of the bodies of his victims were ever found, the charges against him did not include murder. Not long after Murrell was imprisoned, travelers along the Old Sage Road began reporting the sudden appearance of a long, small dog that ran alongside their wagons, apparently looking for her owners. The dog seemed to glow as it ran along. People walking along the road were delighted to find that they were being accompanied by a little white dog that never barked. When they attempted to reach out and pet the dog, she always disappeared.

According to one local legend, a young man was so frightened by the spectral dog that he tried to run away from her. At one point, he became so desperate that he picked up a fence rail and threw it at the dog. To his amazement, the rail passed right through the luminous animal. The young man began running again, with the ghost dog fast on his heels. He finally lost his canine pursuer when he reached a place in the road where the dog always seemed to disappear.

In the twentieth century, people driving along what is now Tennessee Route 46 have reported seeing a short, white dog struggling to keep pace with their speeding vehicles. People continued seeing the little dog until the 1960s. Perhaps the loyal pooch has finally been reunited with her family in the afterlife. One can only hope.

The Fiddlin' Snake Man

Hundreds of legends have been generated by unusual geological formations. A good case in point is New England's Great Stone Face, and Lovers' Leaps can be found throughout the entire country. In a remote part of Johnson County, a rock outcropping known by the locals as Screaming Rock and Fiddler's Rock has given rise to one of East Tennessee's signature ghost stories.

Around the turn of the century, a young man named Martin Stone was known as the best fiddler player in Johnson County. For years, Martin traveled the backroads, playing the old English ballads and reels that he had learned from his grandfather. He made a living playing at weddings, square dances, church picnics, and even funerals. Martin was said to be such an expert fiddle player that he could heal the sick and stop babies from crying. On Sundays when Martin was not required to play, he enjoyed climbing up a stone bluff and playing his fiddle while the sun came up. Sometimes, if he did not have a gig scheduled for that particular day, he continued playing until sundown.

Martin's fiddle playing was put to the test one day. He was sitting on the bluff, playing for no one in particular, when a snake slithered from under a rock and began watching him play. More snakes followed suit, until Martin was completely surrounded by rattlesnakes. As Martin played the old familiar mountain tunes, the reptiles swayed in time with the music. The snakes remained curled up in the sun, enjoying Martin's fiddle playing, until nightfall.

The next Sunday, Martin returned to his post atop the bluff and commenced to play. Once again, the rattlesnakes emerged from their hiding places, curled up, and listened to him. What happened next depends on who is telling the story. Some say that when one of the largest snakes remained on the bluff after the others had left, Martin, on a whim, pinned the snake to the ground with a forked stick and crushed its head under his boot. Others say that after mesmerizing the snakes the first time, Martin realized that he could probably make more money from rattlesnake hides than he could from fiddle playing. So when he returned to the bluff a second time, he proceeded to blast away at the snakes with a shotgun, killing as many as he could carry back home. The demand for rattlesnake hides was so great in Johnson County that Martin began going up to

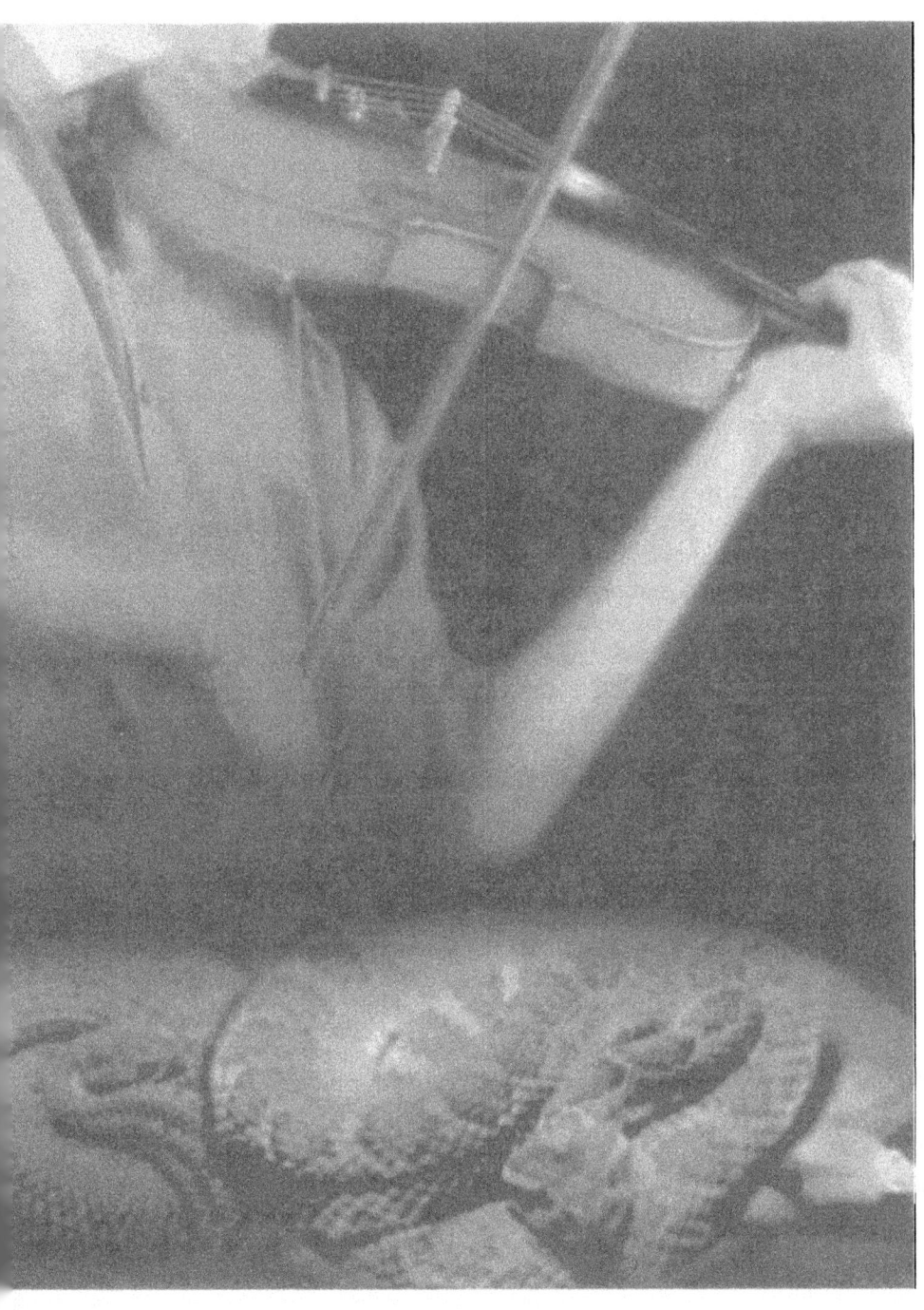

the ledge four or five times a week to kill snakes and fatten his purse. He soon became known far and wide as the Fiddlin' Snake Man.

After several weeks of charming the snakes with his fiddle playing, Martin began to wonder whether the snakes would come out at night. One Sunday, as the sun was going down, Martin took the worn path up to the ledge where he had spent so much time hypnotizing snakes. The next morning, a man riding past the bluff found Martin's mule tethered at the slope. Knowing that Martin never spent all night on the ledge, the man became alarmed. He returned to town and organized a search party. The men had not been on the bluff for very long before they discovered Martin's body. His swollen hands and face were covered with more than two dozen fang marks.

No one really knows how Martin died. Because his bow was found near the round rock where Martin usually sat, the searchers deduced that he had dropped it while he was playing the fiddle, and when he bent down to pick it up, the rattlesnakes stirred from their trance and attacked him. To this day, the residents of Johnson County shun Fiddler's Bluff. They believe that the high-pitched screeching sounds the wind makes as it whistles through the rocks are actually the lilting tones of Martin Stone's fiddling.

Rowena's Restless Spirit and the Hound of Hell

Reverend Frederick A. Ross built Rotherford Mansion on Netherland Inn Road in Kingsport in 1818. The reverend doted on his beautiful daughter Rowena, sending her to the finest schools in the North. She was a charming girl who was courted by men from the most prominent families in Rossville, which later became Kingsport. Two years after she completed her education, she fell in love with a young man from a neighboring town. On the day they were to be married, however, his boat capsized in the Holston River in plain view of Rotherford Mansion. Rowena, who witnessed the drowning of her lover, sank into a deep depression, rarely venturing from her room.

Two years later, Rowena left the security of her home and began attending social functions in Rossville. She became engaged again, this time to a wealthy young man from Knoxville. Shortly before they were to be married, he died of yellow fever. Once again, Rowena became reclusive. Ten years later, Rowena decided to take another chance on love. She married and had a daughter. One day, when the child was six years old, Rowena became convinced that the young man who had drowned in the Holston River was calling her. She walked into the river and drowned herself.

For many years, residents of Kingsport have seen Rowena's ghost, walking along the banks of the river in search of her lost love. The ghost of the young man is said to haunt the mansion as well. In 1995, a man and his family were fishing from the bank of the Holston River near a bridge when they heard laughter. The man looked up from fishing and saw a man and woman, wearing wedding clothes from the previous century, walking down the steps of Rotherford Mansion. The couple seemed to be very much in love. The fisherman turned to his brother to point out the happy couple, but when he looked back, they were gone.

The constant sightings of Rowena's restless spirit made it difficult for her father to recover from his grief. Reverend Ross experienced even more tragedy in 1847, when financial setbacks forced him to sell Rotherwood Mansion to a cruel slaveholder named Joshua Phipps. After the sale, neighbors reported hearing screams coming from the plantation. Rumors soon spread around Rossville that Phipps beat his slaves on a whipping post he had set up inside the mansion. Stories of the torture Phipps inflicted on his slaves gave rise to the rumor that bloodstains that had soaked into the wooden floorboards reappear whenever it rains. As a result of Phipps's alleged abuse of his servants, he was ostracized by the owners of neighboring plantations.

Residents of Kingsport believe that a curse placed on Phipps by his slaves might have been responsible for his death. During the summer of 1861, Phipps contracted a mysterious illness and became bedridden. His only companion at this time was a young slave who fanned him. People say that Phipps died one July morning when a swarm of flies suddenly materialized and filled his mouth and nostrils, suffocating him.

Phipps's notoriety attracted a large crowd to his funeral on July 10. As dark clouds billowed in the sky, the horses pulling the carriage holding the man's casket suddenly had great difficulty surmounting the hill to the graveyard, as if the casket had suddenly became heavier. After struggling for several hours, the horses began to move the carriage. Witnesses say that as streaks of lightning flashed across the sky, a gigantic, black dog leaped from the coffin and ran down the hill. Women screamed and men gasped at the sight of the monstrous dog, which has come to be known as the Hound of Hell. The dog was no sooner out of sight than the sky seemed to open up. While the "mourners" sought shelter from the rain, the gravediggers hastily interred Phipps's corpse.

Phipps's reign of terror at Rotherwood Mansion has given rise to a number of ghost stories. Locals say that on dark, stormy nights, the Hound of Hell's spine-tingling howl resounds through the hills of Kingsport. Apparently the ghost of Phipps still enjoys tormenting people. Subsequent owners of Rotherwood say that a malicious spirit throws back the covers late at night while they are trying to sleep. They have also heard what can best be described as an evil laugh. William Shakespeare's pronouncement that "the evil that men do lives long after their bones have been interred" certainly seems to apply to Joshua Phipps.

The Wampus Cat

In the southeastern United States, the name of Wampus Cat is applied to any large, catlike creature with a loud, shrill cry. In East Tennessee, however, the term predates the arrival of white men in the region. The creature has usually been described as being four feet tall, with a mesmerizing gaze. Wampus Cats feed on rabbits, raccoons, domestic pets, and other small animals. According to Cherokee legends, the Wampus Cat is actually part feline and part human.

As the story goes, hundreds of years ago, a beautiful Indian woman was not content to stay home while her husband and the other men went hunting. She longed to savor the thrill of the hunt, the quickening of the pulse as the hunter discovered fresh deer sign and took off in pursuit of the animal. One day, the woman gave in to her secret desire and followed the men as they went off in search of game. Miraculously, she remained undetected the entire day as the men looked for tracks and sharpened their arrowheads. After sunset, she hid behind a rock, and with a warm mountain lion skin wrapped around her shoulders, she closely observed the men as they told

tribal stories and performed magical rites. She became so absorbed in the men's activities that she accidentally bumped an overhanging tree branch. Thinking that a predator was getting ready to pounce, the men rushed to the rock where the woman was hiding. When they discovered a cowering woman in place of a mountain lion or human enemy, their surprise instantly turned into anger. How dare a woman spy on their sacred tribal rites!

The men consulted the medicine man and asked him to devise a fitting punishment for the woman. Staring at the skin adorning her shoulders, the medicine man decided to bind her to the mountain lion hide forever. He performed a magical spell and changed the woman into an abominable creature, half human and half cat. Giving her the name Wampus Cat, the medicine man cast her out of the camp to roam the hills, desolate and alone.

It has been said that the Wampus Cat's mournful howl can still be heard in the hills of East Tennessee. Some people even claim to have had personal encounters with the mythical beast. On the *American Folklore* website, S. E. Schlosser tells the story of a man who was hunting one night with his dogs when, inexplicably, the animals started whining and ran off. At that same moment, the man's nostrils were assailed by an especially pungent odor, like that of a rotten animal skin. He was standing there, trying to identify the source of the musky smell, when a piercing scream directly behind him caused him to drop his rifle. The man spun around on his heels, and what he saw chilled his blood. Staring at him with saucerlike yellow eyes was a feline creature. The drooling beast resembled a mountain lion except for the fact that it stood on two legs. Without warning, the Wampus Cat howled again. Fear overrode the man's intrinsic curiosity, and he sprinted as fast as he could to a friend's house. His friend looked out the window to see what was causing the commotion outside, and he was astounded by what he saw. He held the front door until the man had dashed inside; then he slammed the door in the face of his pursuer. The creature crashed into the door with such force that it seemed to bounce off its hinges. While the Wampus Cat vented its frustration in a series of horrifying cries, the man's friend tried to repel the creature by grabbing his Bible and reading from the book of Psalms. After a few minutes, the Wampus Cat slunk off into the darkness.

The Wampus Cat has even been sighted in large cities, such as Knoxville. In the early 2000s, a student enrolled at the University of Tennessee had just moved into her new apartment at 16th and Cumberland Streets. It was the first week of school, and she was looking out her window when she saw something that defies belief. At first she thought she was looking at a human being. Then she realized that it was a human-size, catlike being that was walking on its hind legs. The girl distinctly recalled that the beast had glowing, hypnotic eyes. She continued watching the creature until it walked out of sight.

Everyone who has ever encountered the Wampus Cat has paid a high price for the experience in one way or another. Consequences have included the loss of animal life, the loss of one's reputation, and in the most extreme cases, the loss of sanity. In another Cherokee legend, a young brave who tried to drive the Wampus Cat away from his village lost his mind as soon as the beast came into view. Friends and neighbors might arrive at the same conclusion about anyone who claims to have seen the Wampus Cat.

School Spirits

When the Bristol public school system was organized in 1888, administrators were forced to use older buildings as schools. The district rented out the Baptist Academy on Anderson Street as the girls school. Cornfield Academy, the nickname given to an old building on the corner of Anderson and 10th Streets, became the boys school. The first new public school building, which was constructed in 1893 next to King's College on 5th Street, was called Fifth Grade School. This new school, where grades four through ten were taught, had a staff of seven teachers and one principal. The early elementary grades were taught at Cornfield Academy.

The next new building, which was completed on Alabama Street in 1916, housed the first Tennessee High School. The original section of the present-day Tennessee High School, which included the Stone Castle Stadium, was built in 1939 on Edgemont Avenue. Additions to the high school were made in a series of ten-year phases. Following extensive renovation to the main building, an eight-thousand-seat arena was added in 1977. Today Tennessee High School prides itself on its traditions, which include the Class Night ceremony, during which the senior class officially passes down the symbols of the school to the junior class. Another important legacy of Tennessee High School is its three ghost stories.

One of the school's best-known ghosts is that of a former student named Agnes. Many years ago, following the Class Night ceremony, she was on her way to a dance when the car she was riding in was struck by a train at a notoriously dangerous intersection. Agnes was killed instantly. Since that fateful night, her ghost has been seen many times in the original part of the school. Before the corridors were carpeted, students and staff heard ghostly footsteps echoing through the school. Even though no one hears her footsteps anymore, janitors working after hours have felt her presence. Some people have even seen the white figure of a girl passing down the hallways. In *Haunted Tennessee*, Charles Price says that every night at midnight, while rehearsing for an operetta, members of the chorus saw Agnes's ghost float out of the attic and sit on the rail above the clock, usually contentedly swinging her legs. Sightings of Agnes ceased at the same time that the production of operettas and plays was halted.

Another ghost that makes an occasional appearance at the high school is the spirit of an athlete who was walking home from a game one night when he was run over by a car. The athlete apparently was so attached to his school that his ghost is still seen in the field house during games. His ghost is not nearly as well known as the ghost of Agnes, however.

The third ghost that haunts Tennessee High School is not the spirit of a living being. For many years, the spectral image of a nineteenth-century steam engine has been seen rumbling down the hallway before vanishing, usually late at night. The train's ghost is so noisy that the vibrations of the engine have been known to cause the entire building to shake. Locals say that at one time, a railroad passed through the site where the high school is now located.

Hauntings have been an important part of school lore in the United States for years. For many teachers, administrators, janitors, and students, school is more than simply a place to work or learn; it is a world unto itself, a world that is difficult to say good-bye to. And at Tennessee High School, the phrase "school spirit" takes on an entirely new meaning.

The Haunted Jazz Club

The Baker-Peters Jazz Club was originally a house built in 1840 by Dr. James Harvey Baker in the center of a large farm in western Knox County. No one really knows which side Dr. Baker supported during the Civil War. Some people believe that he preferred to remain neutral, but the fact that his son Abner fought for the Confederacy suggests that the doctor's sympathies really lay with the South. In the late 1800s, following the deaths of Dr. Baker and Abner, the old house was sold to the George Peters family. Today, the building is home to the Baker-Peters Jazz Club, an upscale restaurant where customers can dine on fresh seafood or aged Angus beef while enjoying live jazz. However, many people believe that the main attraction at the Baker-Peters Jazz Club has been dead for more than a century.

In June 1863, Dr. Baker was in his yard when a Federal soldier rode up and accused him of harboring Confederate soldiers in his house. According to an article that appeared in the *Knoxville Daily Register* on June 23, 1863, Dr. Baker and the soldier pulled their guns and fired at each other. The doctor ran inside his house while the soldier and several cohorts began firing through the windows on both sides. They demanded that the Confederate soldiers inside the house surrender. Baker went to one of the windows and shouted down to the soldiers that he would surrender if they would cease firing. The Union soldiers began to shoot at him as soon as he stuck his head through the window, however, so he drew his pistol and fired back. The soldiers then ran to the front of the house and smashed open the lower doors.

Once inside the house, they began firing up through the ceiling into the floor of the room where they thought the Bakers were hiding. They then ran up the stairway and ordered Dr. Baker to surrender. Mrs. Baker came out of the room and told the soldiers that her husband would surrender if they promised not to shoot him when he walked through the door. The angry soldiers threatened to shoot Mrs. Baker if she did not move away from the door. Dr. Baker then appeared in the doorway and pulled his wife into the room. The Yankees immediately fired a volley at Baker, inflicting two mortal wounds. As he fell to the floor, the doctor said to his wife, "They have killed me!" Pushing his wife aside, the soldiers proceeded to jab the muzzle of a gun in Dr. Baker's mouth, run a bayonet through his cheek, and strike him in the head. After twenty-two-year-old Abner Baker returned from the war and discovered that his father had been brutally killed in his own home, he shot and killed the man who had informed on his father, Knoxville postmaster William Hall. Abner was arrested, but on September 4, 1865, an angry mob removed the young man from his jail cell and hanged him.

Abner's physical remains lie in the Presbyterian Church cemetery, but many staff members and customers believe that his spirit, and maybe those of other members of his family, have come home to the Baker-Peters Jazz Club. Over the years, there have been reports of poltergeist activity, such as ghostly laughter, strange noises, and lights that turn on by themselves. Hanging in the downstairs hall is a photograph of a blurred figure in an antebellum dress in an upstairs window. The assistant manager of the jazz club, Bob Wilson, says that one day, he was working in his office when he heard a voice calling his name. The voice seemed to be coming from his computer, which does not have a sound chip.

On October 1–2, 2005, two members of the Alternate Realities Center, Stacey Allen McGee and Michael Combs, conducted an investigation of the Baker-Peters Jazz Club. While they were there, the group took photographs of several orbs. They also captured the image of the head and torso of a man in nineteenth-century clothing. Using copper divining rods, Stacey and Michael asked the entities yes-no questions. Stacey encouraged a ghost that called itself Abner to go to the light. They also contacted the spirits of a female servant and someone who visited the house years ago.

Like many haunted restaurants, the Baker-Peters Jazz Club has accepted its ghostly inhabitant. The club even promotes its ghost on its website. Ghosts, it seems, can do more than simply terrify observers. They can be good for business.

Lydia's Ghost

The Greenbrier Restaurant is one of Gatlinburg's most popular eateries. Its main log structure was built in 1939, when it was known as the Greenbrier Lodge. The owner, Mrs. Blanche Moffett, served breakfast to the hunters and travelers who were attracted to the lodge's secluded woodland setting, its sundeck, and the first concrete swimming pool in Gatlinburg. In 1980, Dean and Barbara Hayden bought the lodge and renamed it the Greenbrier Restaurant. The restaurant was leased out before Dean died in 1991. Two years later, Barbara appointed her son David and his wife, Becky, as managers and reopened the restaurant. Today the Greenbrier Restaurant is owned and operated by David, Becky, and their son Jordan. The food and the ambience still attract customers, much as they did back in 1939. These days, though, the Greenbrier's ghost story also brings people to the restaurant.

Legend has it that in the 1940s, a young woman named Lydia was staying at the lodge. Her fiancé was a handsome young man who lived in Gatlinburg. On the day of her wedding, she put on her bridal gown in the lodge and drove to the church where she was to be married. After six hours of waiting, she reached the unmistakable conclusion that her lover had jilted her. Despondent, she returned to the lodge, where she walked up the stairs to the second-floor landing. The poor girl threw a rope over the rafters, tied the end around her neck, and hanged herself. A few days later, hunters discovered the mangled corpse of her fiancé. He had apparently been attacked and killed by a mountain lion. It was not long before locals speculated that Lydia's spirit had taken the shape of a mountain lion and wrought revenge on the man who had dishonored her.

Today, Lydia's ghost seems to be a very active presence at the restaurant. Lydia usually haunts the second-floor landing where she jumped to her death, although customers have also reported seeing her wander through the restaurant. On the *Ghosts of Tennessee* website, D. L. Marsh says that according to a caretaker who worked at the lodge many years ago, he was awakened from his sleep one night by a female voice that told him, "Mark my grave." He dismissed the voice as a figment of his imagination and went back to sleep. After several sleepless nights, the caretaker decided to honor Lydia's request. He walked down to the hill where Lydia was said to have been buried and placed a cross on her grave. Lydia's ghost never bothered him again.

When the Haydens bought the restaurant in 1980, several family members lived in the old lodge because they had not found a house yet. "My husband's brother thought he heard his father downstairs," Becky says. "He went downstairs to check and found all the chairs were pushed over to the wall and stacked up. They were big, heavy, wrought-iron chairs. His brother thought his dad had come home, but he looked out the window, and the car wasn't back. So he straightened everything up and went back upstairs. When he came down a while later, everything had been stacked up again, so they left it."

Once the restaurant was fully operational, customers began to have bizarre experiences there. One day, when a regular customer was in the ladies' restroom, the light went off and then came back on a few seconds later. A little while later, the same lady and her husband were talking to some people in the restaurant when she decided to use the restroom again. "Apparently, something went into the restroom with the lady," says Becky, "and went into the stall right beside hers and slammed the toilet seat down. 'Bam! Bam!' The husband was sitting on the bench outside the door. He heard it too." Afterward, the lady's husband accused Becky of having rigged up a device that would cause the toilet seat to slam down on its own or turn the lights off and on. Becky denied the accusation. "Nobody touched it. I promise you. It must be Lydia."

When their son Jordan was little, Becky and her husband had a room upstairs where the office is now. "It had a TV and a couch so he could take a nap if he wanted to," Becky says. "After school, he'd go up there and do his homework while we were down here in the restaurant. Several times, he said he saw a lady up there, but we knew there was no lady there. Sometimes we would all be downstairs, and we'd hear footsteps coming from upstairs when there was nobody up there. There were people who would say they saw a lady at the top of the stairs who would walk into that room."

In November 2003, Jordan saw Lydia's ghost a second time. "We were behind and short-handed," Becky says, "and we closed on Monday to get caught up. Well, I was out here doing a liquor order, and my husband was back in the kitchen prepping food. Jordan was back there watching TV. He kept yelling for me to come to the back. I told him, 'I'm busy.' About the third or fourth time, he hollered really loud. When I went back there, he said, 'There was a girl standing beside me, and now she's gone. She was just standing there, and she disappeared.' I asked, 'What did she look like?' He said, 'I don't know. She was kind of foggy.'"

During the winter of 2004, Becky had an encounter with what was likely the same apparition. "I got here early one morning," she says. "There was nobody else here. It was maybe 10:30, and we propped the restroom doors open. We also propped the doors open to the service area. I know there was no one here but me. All of a sudden, all of the doors popped open. There was nobody here. You could hear the trucks drive by. There are no windows in the front area, so there's no light unless you turn the light on. I walked across the threshold to turn the light on, and I ran into somebody. It took my breath away. I said, 'Excuse me,' but there was nobody here but me. It was very strange, but I felt like I ran into somebody. I turned off the lights and came back in here to pay the beer man. I went ahead and got my check filled out as best I could. It's not scary. It's not threatening. It's like all the hairs on the back of your neck stand up."

Becky says that on several occasions, she or her husband got to the bottom of the hill after closing up, only to remember something that they had forgotten at the restaurant. When they went back up into the dark, empty restaurant, they heard strange noises or had the hairs on the back of the neck stand up. "No one wanted to be the last person to shut off the lights and be the last one in the building," Becky says.

The staff at the Greenbrier Restaurant has also had strange experiences in the old restaurant. According to a hostess named Christine Kauffman, she was turning out the lights one night when she heard something. "It sounded like a laminated menu," Christine says. "I turned around, and nothing was behind me. Well, I continued to turn off the lights, because there's a lot of stuff to turn off. I turned around again, and nothing was there. It sounded just like this." She shakes one of the laminated menus. "I could also feel the wind from it. I went back to turn off the lights, and as I was coming back around, there was a menu lying on the floor."

One winter night, Christine and another hostess named Marie heard someone walking around on the second floor. They assumed that it was Jordan, because he spent a lot of time up there. The girls mentioned hearing the footsteps to Becky, and she too assumed that Jordan was up there. At that moment, Jordan came walking out of the office. Nobody—at least, nobody human—was up on the second floor.

Finding out about the ghosts at the Greenbrier Restaurant is not difficult at all. Simply sit at the bar, order a drink, and talk to the bartender and people sitting nearby. On the day my wife, Marilyn, and her friend Vickie Hatcher were there, an attendant at the Welcome Center in Sevierville told them that he was sitting at the bar at the Greenbrier Restaurant when out of the corner of his eye, he saw someone rush past him. He found this incident to be highly unusual because he and the bartender were the only ones there at the time. But it seems that at the Greenbrier Restaurant, occurrences that would be extraordinary anywhere else are just run-of-the-mill.

The UFOs of Oak Ridge

The creation of the city of Oak Ridge was predicted by John Hendrix—an eccentric local resident regarded as a mystic—forty years before its founding. In 1942, Major General Leslie Groves chose the rural site as the location for developing materials for the Manhattan Project. Late in 1942, two plants were built in Oak Ridge for the purpose of separating uranium 235 from natural uranium. A permanent town was built at the end of the valley to accommodate the large number of workers who would be participating in the project. Before the end of World War II, the population of Oak Ridge had swelled to seventy thousand people. Oak Ridge was shifted to civilian control in 1947. For a few days in October 1950, however, it seemed that UFOs were taking over the new town.

The first encounter took place on October 13, when Atomic Energy Commission Security Patrol Trooper Edward D. Rymer and John Moneymaker, a caretaker from the University of Tennessee Agricultural Research Farm, observed some sort of aircraft making an outside loop about twelve thousand to fifteen thousand feet above Solway Gate in the "control zone." The pear-shaped object, which left behind a distinct vapor trail, went into a dive and then slowly flew parallel to the ground. When Trooper Rymer walked toward the object, it suddenly shrank in size and began moving southeast. In a complex series of maneuvers, the object managed to clear a nine-foot chain-link fence, a willow tree, and telephone lines before soaring over a hill a mile away. Joe Zarzecki, captain of the Atomic Energy Commission Security Patrol, also saw the unidentified flying object, and his description matches those given by Rymer and Moneymaker.

On October 20 at 3:27 P.M., a pilot with the 5th AW-Fighter Squad was sent on a mission to investigate a radar sighting of several "targets." He radioed back that the objects were between eighteen and twenty-five miles away from the Knoxville Airport. He was unable to identify any of the objects.

Another eyewitness reported seeing a UFO at 4:55 P.M. on October 20. Larry P. Riordan, the superintendent of security in the control zone, was driving on the road to the Oak Ridge agricultural farm when he saw a balloonlike object directly above the University of Tennessee Agricultural Research Farm. Something seemed to be hanging below the bottom of the object. The "balloon," which was gunmetal gray in color and between eight and ten feet long, hovered about a quarter mile away from Riordan. He said that as he drove around a curve, the object seemed to grow thinner. Riordan saw his UFO at exactly the same time that the Air Force pilot saw his.

On October 23, an unidentified man was driving on the Benton Valley Road when he saw an object flying between one thousand and two thousand feet above the Scarboro School, which is within the control zone. He described the object as an aluminum flash, which was moving southeast at first. After it crossed the road, it went into a rapid descent and noiselessly disappeared over the ridge. At the same time, a Geiger counter in the area registered a reading for alpha and beta particles.

On October 24 at 6:45 P.M., William B. Fry, assistant chief of security, was watching a movie at a drive-in theater with his family when he noticed a flying object moving back and forth horizontally within thirty degrees of his line of sight. The color of the glowing object changed from red to green, to blue-green, to blue, and then to orange. Fry's wife and the projectionist also saw the object. Ten minutes later, Air Force major Lawrence Ballweg observed the same flying object from his house. He continued watching it until it disappeared at 7:20 P.M.

The four-day sightings in Oak Ridge are still a mystery. The declassified FBI reports from which this information was taken took care to point out that most of the witnesses were level-headed individuals who worked as either military or security personnel. The Security Division of Oak Ridge, the Air Force Radar and Fighter Squadrons, and the FBI rejected the possible explanations of insect swarms, flights of birds, flying kites, objects thrown from the ground, mass hysteria, balloons of any description, and practical jokers. The more imaginative residents of Oak Ridge wonder whether alien visitors were attracted to the "Atomic City" because of the role it played in the Manhattan Project only a few years before.

Black Aggie

When the Scotch-Irish immigrated to the American South in the early nineteenth century, they brought along with them stories of ghosts and witches from their homeland. One of the legends that Scottish grandparents told their grandchildren late at night in front of the flickering warmth of the fireplace is the tale of Black Aggie, a blue-skinned woman from the Scottish Highlands who ate people. Once the story was transported to the United States, it became the tale of a woman who had the unfortunate reputation of being a witch. Shunned by all her neighbors, the woman died, dejected and alone. Supposedly her ghost haunts the cemetery in which she was buried. She is a vengeful spirit with red eyes glowing from the sockets of a skeletal face. She eats people who are brave—or foolish— enough to venture into the graveyard at night. One of the cemeteries in East Tennessee that she is reputed to haunt is the Old Gray Cemetery near Knoxville.

Named in honor of the British poet Thomas Gray, Old Gray Cemetery was incorporated in 1850, but the cemetery was not dedicated until June 1, 1852. The site now encompasses 13.47 acres and is bounded by Broadway, Tyson, and Cooper Streets. To date, there have been fifty-seven hundred burials in the cemetery since it was founded. The elaborately shaped and carved monuments clearly mark this as a Victorian cemetery.

Teenagers in the area seem to believe that Black Aggie hides among the tombstones and monuments in the Old Gray Cemetery. In the early 1990s, two young men drove out to the cemetery in hopes of taking a picture of a ghost with their Polaroid camera. After walking around the tombstones for a few minutes, the boys grew tired of ghost hunting and climbed back into the car. While the boys were drinking beer, they began hurling epithets at the ghosts.

The boys had drunk several cans of beer when one of them left the car to urinate. He was relieving himself by a memorial statue when he noticed a black, gelatinous substance oozing from one of the cracks. Gradually the substance formed the amorphous image of a human being. When the thing began moving toward the boy, he ran away as fast as he could without tripping over the tombstones. After he made it to the car, he threw open the door and yelled at his friend, "Go! Go!" As the car was backing out of the cemetery, one of the boys allegedly managed to take a photograph of the entity. No one besides the two boys has ever seen the picture, however.

Granted, most of the stories told about Black Aggie have probably been fabricated by teenage boys as a means of scaring their buddies or girlfriends. Indeed, in *Haints, Witches, and Boogers*, Charles Edwin Price recounts the attempt of a young man to frighten his girlfriend by jumping out from behind a tombstone dressed in cheesecloth and a fright mask. Ironically, the young prankster was scared by a friend of his girlfriend's, who had dressed up like Black Aggie. Stories like these just go to show that there is probably more fantasy than fact in the fantastic stories passed down about Black Aggie.

Terror in the Tunnels

Sullivan County has two abandoned tunnels that are said to be haunted. Click Tunnel, on Sensabaugh Hollow Road in Church Hill, was originally a natural tunnel that was widened by the Clinchfield Railroad when it laid tracks in the 1920s. Sensabaugh Tunnel, off Big Elm Road in Kingsport, was cut by Sensabaugh Branch. In the 1920s, sixteen men died when the tunnel was being widened. Because the two tunnels are so close to each other, they share the same ghost stories.

According to one legend, a slave woman who had borne three of her master's children sought refuge in the natural tunnel. She was planning to wait for a ferryman to come down the Holston River and pick her up. When the slaveowner finally tracked the woman to the tunnel, he was so angry that he grabbed the youngest child and slammed its head against the tunnel wall. He then pulled out his pistol and shot the slave woman and their other two children. The site of this story is probably Click Tunnel.

Another legend has it that years ago, a vagrant stopped at a farmhouse not far from Sensabaugh Tunnel. He offered to chop wood in exchange for a hot meal. In *More Haunted Tennessee*, Charles Edwin Price writes that while the man was eating dinner, he noticed a silver cup that appeared to be valuable. He tried to hide the cup in his clothes, but the farmer saw him and ran for his pistol. Meanwhile, the vagrant picked up the baby sleeping in a cradle and ran out the door. He had intended to use the infant as a shield, but by the time he arrived at the tunnel, he decided that the baby would just slow him down. The desperate man dropped the baby in the creek that flows through the tunnel and drowned it.

In a third variant, a young, unmarried woman walked into Click Tunnel to have her baby. She was in the throes of labor when her father arrived. Insane with rage, the man stood by until the baby was born. He then picked up the newborn infant and drowned it in the creek.

The fourth version has a woman who was heading with her baby to Church Hill and drove into Click Tunnel to escape a downpour. She was trying to wait out the storm with the engine running, when suddenly the car died. The next morning, she and the infant were found dead in the car.

The last version of the story concerns Mr. Sensabaugh, whose house was located within one hundred yards of the west end of the tunnel. One night, Sensabaugh went insane and killed his entire family, including his newborn son. He dragged their bodies to the tunnel and tossed their corpses into the creek.

A common thread running through all five stories is the death of a baby. All of the stories end with the baby's mournful cry, which passersby still claim to hear. People have also heard phantom footsteps, voices, and screams inside the tunnel. It is also said that if people drive inside the tunnel and turn off their engines, their cars will not start again. Locals who are bold enough to test the veracity of the legends have parked their cars inside the tunnels and observed in their rearview mirrors a shadowy form walking toward their vehicles. Occasionally, curiosity seekers who turn off their engines feel their vehicles rocking back and forth. When they return home and climb out of their vehicles, they notice small handprints on the side panels. In 2003, a young man and two of his friends drove their pickup truck inside Sensabaugh Tunnel and turned off the engine. Suddenly they saw a light moving toward them from the end of the tunnel. The driver attempted to start the truck, but the engine stalled. Looking over his shoulder, he noticed that the light had dropped into the creek and disappeared. On his second attempt to ignite the engine, it started, and the terrified boys sped out of the tunnel.

In October 2006, *Haunted South TV*, a syndicated program that airs in Tennessee and several other states, conducted a scientific investigation of Sensabaugh Tunnel. Using sound-wave imagery, the team photographed a disturbance that resembled a woman walking down the tunnel. The team also caught the image of a moving orb on film.

The ghosts of crying babies are staples of local folklore in many isolated communities in the South. Because the tales take place in out-of-the-way locations, young people who drive out there to party are the primary transmitters of the legends. Folklorists are not at all surprised that the abandoned tunnels in Sullivan County have generated such a large number of stories, not just because of their remoteness, but also because tunnels are, by their nature, very creepy places.

Long Island Legends

Long Island, Tennessee, is a far cry from its much more famous counterpart, Long Island, New York. This four-mile-long, half-mile-wide island in the Holston River was sacred to the Cherokee Indians, who held sacred rituals and made sacrifices there. It was also a place where parleys called "talk-talks" were held with tribes who had trespassed on their hunting grounds. Even though the Cherokees believed that revenge was a noble virtue, tribal law prevented the killing of anyone on their sacred island, including whites. But the tranquility of Long Island was shattered in 1777, and perhaps forever after, when an Indian curse transformed the island into a violent, bloody place.

When whites began settling Kentucky and Middle Tennessee, Long Island became strategically important because of its location just east of the junction of the North and South Forks of the Holston River. On March 10, 1775, Daniel Boone, along with thirty axmen, began work on the Wilderness Trail at Long Island. Colonial settlement in East Tennessee led the Cherokees to assist the British during the Revolutionary War. In July 1776, the Cherokees attacked the frontiersmen. The defenders of Eaton's Fort retaliated by marching into Long Island Flats and defeating the Cherokees.

On July 20, 1777, the legendary Cherokee chief Atakullakulla signed a treaty with white soldiers that required the Indians to give up their claims to lands settled by whites in East Tennessee. The Treaty of Long Island also forced the Cherokees to relinquish Long Island to the whites. Not all of the Cherokees were satisfied with the treaty, however. The story goes that as the Cherokees were leaving their lands, a medicine man cursed Long Island, proclaiming that no white men would ever be able to live there in peace.

For more than two hundred years, as the medicine man predicted, murder and madness have afflicted the residents of Long Island. Many people have been killed there. The most famous murders were committed in 1925, when a fugitive named Kinnie Wagner gunned down the law enforcement officers who had been dispatched to arrest him. One of the murders on Long Island has become the stuff of legend. In the early 1940s, a resident of Kingsport whom folklorist Charles Edwin Price has identified as Albert Ross discovered that his son, who was on leave from the U.S. Marines, had driven to a local make-out spot on Long Island with his girlfriend. A devout Christian, Ross decided to intervene before his son committed a mortal sin. When Ross arrived at a secluded spot on the island, he was shocked to find the pair in the throes of passion. Before the startled couple could rise from the ground, Ross attacked them. Mad with rage, he began stabbing his son with a long knife. In another version of the tale, he beat his son with a tree limb. After his son had slipped into unconsciousness, Ross killed his son's girlfriend. Dropping his weapon, Ross disappeared into the darkness, never to be seen again.

Not surprisingly, Long Island has gained a reputation as a very haunted place. It is said that any couples bold enough to venture out to the island for some "private time" have been terrified by the sight of a wild-eyed, wild-haired man, wielding a club or a knife and running in their direction. Price says that the flickering campfires of the Cherokees can still be seen on the island. People riding down the Holston River claim to have heard the chanting of Cherokee warriors echoing through the night. Occasionally ghostly canoes are seen gliding down the river.

No one lives on Long Island today. Half of the island has been turned into a park by the city of Kingsport, and the other half is occupied by a waste treatment plant. Maybe it is just as well that there are no permanent residents on Long Island anymore.

ETSU's Haunted Halls

When East Tennessee State University first opened its doors in Johnson City in 1911, it was a training school for teachers. ETSU still prepares teachers for preschool through grade twelve, but it also serves Northeast Tennessee's health-care system, government agencies, and the general public. Sometimes, though, the university's role as the region's primary institution of higher education is eclipsed by its reputation as Tennessee's most haunted university.

Sidney Gilbreath, the founding president of the university, is said to haunt the building named after him, Gilbreath Hall. In his ten years as president, Gilbreath battled with the state legislature and even some of the faculty, but ETSU grew under his stewardship. He apparently remains there today as a vigilant spirit who turns off lights and shuts doors and windows that are carelessly left open. One of the janitors working in the building describes the ghost as a "fussy custodian." Students say that he is often found on the dormitory's top floor, which can be accessed only through a janitors' closet on the floor below.

Students enrolled in computer, math, science, and drama classes in Gilbreath Hall occasionally have what can best be described as paranormal experiences. One young woman was working in the computer lab late one night when all of the computers crashed simultaneously. When the lab assistant jokingly credited the resident ghost with the interruption, the girl felt a cold presence pass by her desk. She never returned to that particular computer lab again. Other students working in the computer lab have seen a male apparition who bears a strong resemblance to Sidney Gilbreath. A group of investigators called the Tri-Area Paranormal Research Group detected a cold spot near the catwalk doors overlooking Gilbreath Theater.

Another campus personality who is said to haunt ETSU is Christine Burleson. A graduate of the normal school, Christine went on to earn master's degrees from Columbia and Oxford Universities. Afterward, Christine returned to ETSU, where she taught courses in Shakespeare for many years. When she was in her sixties, she became confined to a wheelchair after contracting a debilitating disease. Concerned that she would eventually become a burden to her loved ones, Christine shot herself in the head in the early 1970s.

Christine's ghost seems to have taken up residence in the build-ing named after her, Burleson Hall. For one month in 1988, a fac-ulty member heard unsettling moaning sounds in his office. Over the years, the story has arisen that Christine's ghost inhabits the portrait of her father, David Sinclair Burleson, on the second floor. Supposedly the artist modeled David's eyes after Christine's. Some-times people who gaze at the portrait sense that the eyes follow them around. During a late-night investigation of the building, the Tri-Area Paranormal Research Group captured the image of what they described as a "shadow person" on the second floor.

Mathes Hall seems to be haunted as well. Custodians walking the halls at night have heard disembodied footsteps walking right behind them. Whenever they stop walking, the entity following them stops as well. In *Haints, Witches, and Boogers*, Charles Edwin Price tells the story of a female custodian who was taking a break in the janitors' closet when she heard a loud crashing sound from the floor above. She climbed the stairs and walked down the hall-way, but found nothing out of order. The custodian returned to the closet and had just sat down when she heard the crashing sound a second time. Terror-stricken, she called a friend and talked to her on the phone until quitting time. The identity of the ghost roaming Mathes Hall has never been determined.

Lucille Clement Hall, the women's dormitory on the west end of campus, is also thought to be haunted by an unknown spirit. Many residents of the dorm have heard the sound of marbles dropping on the hallway floor, especially at night when they were trying to sleep. They have also heard a little boy playing in deserted hallways. Stu-dents tell the tale of a little boy who was trapped just before the foundation was laid. He tried to alert the workers by throwing mar-bles, but no one heard him. The child was buried in cement, and his body has never been recovered. His ghost still tries to attract the attention of people in the building to this day. In another version of the story, the child was playing at the work site when he dropped one of his marbles. He reached out to grab the marble, lost his foot-ing, and plummeted off the building to his death.

Apparently the boy's spirit has a mischievous streak. One girl says that she heard someone breathing in the bathroom while she was taking a shower. She quickly opened the shower curtain in hopes of catching the intruder unaware, but no one was there. She stepped back into the stall and resumed her shower, but a few minutes later, she heard the breathing again. Once again, when she looked, no one was there. After she finished her shower, the girl reached for her clothes and discovered that they were no longer hung up, but were lying in the hallway. The playful ghost also toys with electrical appliances. A resident named Hailey Wix says that once in a while, the ghost turns off her magnifying mirror. One time, a rapping sound came from the mirror. After Hailey unplugged the mirror, the rapping sound stopped. Another student, Bethany Eldrige, had heated a plate of lasagna and had just set her meal on the bed when, all of a sudden, the plate flipped upside down and onto the floor.

The most haunted building on campus was said to have been Cooper Hall, which was originally a private residence owned by a wealthy businessman named George Carter. Carter, who donated the land on which ETSU was founded, had a daughter named Alice. The lonely girl fell in love with a local boy, but her parents refused to allow them to marry. Despondent, Alice committed suicide by ingesting rat poison. Wracked with guilt, Carter installed a stained-glass portrait of his daughter in his mansion. After Carter died in 1936, the university purchased the house and converted it into a dormitory for senior girls. Before long, residents complained of hearing singing in the halls and screaming during the night. When missing objects turned up after a few days, the girls blamed the prank on the ghost of Alice Carter. They also spread stories of her ghost peeking through the doors to their rooms at night. Ironically, a Johnson City historian who was conducting research on the hauntings in the dormitory discovered that the Carters actually had a son, not a daughter, and that he was the model for the stained-glass portrait. The dormitory was razed in 1984, ostensibly because it had deteriorated beyond repair, but according to the rumor mill, the administration destroyed the old mansion because no one wanted to live there.

Incredibly, Eastern Tennessee State University has never offered any workshops or seminars on the paranormal. In 2007, however, a group of ETSU students formed a paranormal research group called Ghost Walkers, which has been officially recognized as a university organization. Unlike many ghost hunter groups, which travel hundreds of miles in search of active sites, Ghost Walkers does not have very far to go.

What Is Really Shut Up inside Swingle Hospital?

In local folklore, abandoned hospitals are perfect breeding grounds for ghosts, most likely because so many people died there. Not surprisingly, what is believed to be one of the most haunted sites in the entire United States—the Waverly Hills Tuberculosis Sanitorium in Louisville, Kentucky—is a hospital that has been closed since 1961. Most of the ghost stories connected with these creepy buildings have been produced by generations of teenagers who defy the No Trespassing signs in an effort to catch a glimpse of a ghost. The most legendary abandoned hospital in East Tennessee is Swingle Hospital in Johnson City.

The legends surrounding Swingle Hospital are so fantastic that they are most likely apocryphal. The story goes that Dr. Swingle was an incompetent surgeon who practiced in Johnson City in the 1920s. Even though most of the procedures he performed were relatively minor, the majority of his patients died on the operating table. To hide his mistakes, Dr. Swingle buried the corpses in the backyard. Today Swingle Hospital is off-limits to curiosity seekers. After a fire broke out in the building, it was boarded up, and No Trespassing signs were posted. Supposedly the people who live behind Swingle Hospital now own the property. They are very tight-lipped people who refuse to discuss the ghosts with visitors.

It is said that if you walk up the front walkway to the main entrance, you can hear the voices of Dr. Swingle and his assistants. And if you walk around the back of the building, you can hear the cries of the victims of his botched operations. Young people dead set on investigating the truthfulness of the legends claim that when they broke into the old building, they found medical books, magazines, manuals, surgical instruments, and tangled sheets scattered all over the floor. A number of rusty old file cabinets were stored in the basement. Some interlopers claim to have caught orbs in photographs taken inside the old hospital. They have also detected cold spots and hot spots in the house. One young woman who walked around the back of the hospital felt herself being overcome with emotion.

The actual history of Swingle Hospital is much less intriguing than the legends that young people in Johnson City tell about it. In the early 1940s, Dr. Edward Thurston Brading, who had been practicing medicine out west, returned to East Tennessee with the intention of setting up a clinic in Johnson City. Over the next few weeks, Dr. Brading set about recruiting physicians who would be interested in working in a Mayo Clinic style doctor's office. Responding to Brading's job offer were Dr. Carroll H. Long, Dr. Jack Gordon, and Dr. Hugh F. Swingle. Dr. Gordon's father, L. E. Gordon, loaned the doctors money to buy the Adam Crouch property on North Roan Street. Once the clinical operation was up and running, the four doctors were joined by a pediatrician from Charleston, South Carolina, named Dr. Owen Ravenel.

The doctors' partnership ended after two years. Dr. Long had to leave the group to complete his board certification at Bowman Gray School of Medicine. Dr. Gordon left soon thereafter. After Dr. Ravenel's departure, Dr. Brading and Dr. Swingle tried to run the clinic on their own, but after a few weeks, the only doctor left in the hospital was Dr. Swingle. He tried to run the clinic on his own under the name Swingle Hospital, but a staph infection and his inability to attract another partner forced him to close the clinic in the early 1950s. Dr. Swingle then went to work at the local VA hospital and at several institutions at Mountain Home, Tennessee, and in North Carolina. He eventually died of colon cancer.

Most of the legends of Swingle Hospital can be easily refuted. First of all, the hospital opened in the 1940s, not the 1920s, as many locals believe. Elderly people who were patients of Dr. Swingle's remember him as a kindly and very skilled surgeon. Because the white boards that seal up the windows and doors are very thick, it is unlikely than anyone has been able to break into the old hospital. But until the owners allow a bona fide scientific investigation to be conducted at Swingle Hospital, the legends will most likely continue to grow.

Ghostly Guests at Prospect Hill

The Victorian shingle-style brick house in Mountain City that is now Prospect Hill Bed and Breakfast Inn was built in 1889 of handmade brick by Joseph Wagner, who served as a major in the Union Army during the Civil War. Wagner was a prosperous businessman who profited greatly from his mining and mercantile interests. In 1910, the house was purchased by the Rambo family, who brought the house into the twentieth century with plumbing, electricity, and central heating on the first floor. After being occupied by three generations of Rambos, the house was sold in August 1991 to the Cornett family.

A few years later, Robert and Judy Hotchkiss of Atlanta purchased the house with the intention of converting it into a bed-and-breakfast. The experience Robert and Judy had gained from renovating several Victorian houses served them well as they set about updating the six-thousand-square-foot mansion. They christened the old house Prospect Hill in recognition of Major Wagner's mining interests in the area. Before Robert and Judy opened up Prospect Hill as a bed-and-breakfast, they added modern baths to the five guest bedrooms, put in new electrical and plumbing systems, and installed central heat and air-conditioning on the second and third floors. It was after the old house was completely renovated in the late 1990s that they realized that the structural changes in the building might have awakened an otherworldly presence.

Guests at Prospect Hill Bed and Breakfast are treated to whirlpool tubs, clock radios with CD players, scented candles—and, some say, ghostly visitors. Many people have smelled freshly baked peanut butter cookies at 3 A.M. They have also heard the disembodied crying of a baby and the slamming of the laundry room door. Brides who have had wedding receptions at the inn have been shocked to find orbs in their wedding pictures. Photographs taken in front of the fireplace on days when no fires were made reveal tongues of flame curling up behind the screen. One day, two glasses in the bathroom inexplicably exploded. Several years ago, a woman walked into the inn and saw a spectral Civil War soldier staring out the front window. On another occasion, a guest caught a glimpse of a shadowy figure walking around the corner.

One of the most common spooky sounds heard at the inn is the heavy walking of a person wearing leather-soled shoes. In *Haunted Inns of the Southeast*, Sheila Turnage says Judy told her that one day in the summer of 1998, not long after she and her husband had moved in, she heard footsteps walking from the hallway outside the door of her room to the back hall. A few days later, the former owners of the house admitted that they not only had heard ghostly footsteps, but also had seen doors open and close by themselves.

Prospect Hill Bed and Breakfast Inn certainly fulfills its promise of providing its guests with a picturesque getaway. From atop the summit of Prospect Hill, guests can look out the windows of the inn and see three states: North Carolina, Virginia, and Tennessee. And the testimony of guests and staff suggests that some visitors also catch a glimpse of the "other side."

The Helpful Highway Ghost

Highway ghosts are fairly common in Tennessee. The Bristol Highway is said to be haunted by the long dog, a family pet that was brutally killed by the notorious outlaw John Murrell. People traveling along the old stagecoach road near Blountville claim to have seen a man on horseback riding up to the door of the historic Sturm Cabin. On the stretch of I-40 that crosses the Cumberland Mountains, drivers have seen glowing balls of light buzzing around their cars. The best-known haunted road in upper East Tennessee is the Netherland Inn Road near Kingsport.

According to the legend, one foggy night in 1922, five young men were joyriding in a Model T Ford down Rogersville Pike near Rotherwood Bridge when a dog ran in front of the car. The driver swerved to miss the little animal and inadvertently crashed into the concrete abutment of the bridge. When rescuers arrived on the scene, two of the boys were already dead, and another young man died shortly after being admitted to Riverview Hospital. Hugh Hamblen, the father of one of the boys—Charlie—rushed to the hospital as soon as a nurse informed him of the accident. Driving through the fog was difficult, but Hugh still managed to make it to the hospital in less than half an hour. As he parked along the Netherland Inn Road and walked up the hill to the hospital, Hugh feared the worst. When he rushed to Charlie's bedside, Hugh was relieved to find that his son was still alive, although the boy had suffered a concussion and internal injuries. Hugh stayed by his son's bedside the entire night.

The next morning, Hugh was glad to learn that Charlie's condition had improved, but he was saddened by the news that the other survivor of the accident had passed away during the night. With a prayer of thanksgiving on his lips, Hugh left the hospital and walked down the road to his car. He was surprised that the fog from the night before had become thicker. As he was crossing the road to his vehicle, he saw two large, round headlights driving straight toward him. Before he could react, Hugh was struck by the oncoming car. The driver was a girl who had never driven a car before. Hugh was carried back up to the hospital, where he lingered for two days with a crushed chest and pierced lungs. Legend has it that at the very moment Hugh died, Charlie's ears began to bleed. Charlie Hamblen recovered physically from his injuries, but the nagging feeling that he was somehow responsible for his father's death transformed the fun-loving boy into a sullen, morose man.

A few years later, a man was driving down the Netherland Inn Road one foggy night when he saw the figure of a man standing along the roadside. The man was about forty years old and was wearing a trench coat, fedora hat, and white scarf. Suddenly he stepped into the middle of the road and started waving his arms. The driver attempted to stop, but his tires slid on the wet pavement, and his car struck the man. Terrified, he pulled off the road and walked back to the spot where the man had been standing, but no one was there. Since 1922, more than 120 people have reported seeing an apparition standing in the middle of the road, waving his arms. Usually he appears on stormy, misty nights when visibility is poor. Many of these drivers are workers at the nearby Eastman Kodak plant. Hugh Hamblen's ghost, it seems, is a watchful spirit who tries to prevent people from becoming victims of the fog, as he was.

The Watauga River Bridge Phantom

From a historical viewpoint, Elizabethton is one of the most important and fascinating small towns in Tennessee. Originally called the Watauga Settlement at Sycamore Shoals, it was the first permanent settlement outside of the original thirteen colonies. In addition, the first majority-rule system of American democracy was established at Sycamore Shoals. A number of prominent legislators, military leaders, and members of the Constitutional Convention came from this area. In 1780, eleven hundred volunteers, now known as the Overmountain Men, mustered at Sycamore Shoals and started a fourteen-day march to South Carolina, where they fought the British at the Battle of King's Mountain. The town is also known as the launching point for westward expansion.

In the early twentieth century, the name of the town was changed to Elizabethton in honor of Elizabeth MacLin Carter. Elizabethton is home to a number of historic sites, including the Jon and Landon Carter Mansion, the downtown historic district, and a reconstruction of Fort Watauga. For visitors interested in the paranormal, however, the most interesting site in Elizabethton is an old bridge built in the 1920s, the Watauga River Bridge.

The haunting of the Watauga River Bridge is thought to be based on an incident that allegedly took place in the 1930s. One night, a local couple, identified by John Norris Brown on the *Ghosts & Spirits of Tennessee* website as Tom Jackson and Wanda Smithson, drove out to the secluded area, which had become Elizabethton's "Lover's Lane." They had parked their car on the bridge and were enjoying the moonlight, the cool night breezes, and each other's company when Tom noticed a dark figure walking in their direction. In one version of the tale, the interloper was a deranged killer, bent on claiming new victims. In another, he was a robber who stole the couple's valuables.

The stranger's motives might vary from one tale to the next, but the outcome was always the same. As soon as he reached the car, he pulled a knife out from under his coat and began stabbing Wanda. Once Wanda stopped struggling, the killer turned his attention to her boyfriend. Tom was stabbed several times, but somehow he found the strength and will to run away. At that very moment, a man was about to drive his car across the bridge. Frantically waving his arms, Tom stopped the car and climbed in, frightening the woman who was sitting in the backseat. As soon as the driver saw the psychotic murderer marching toward the car with blood dripping from his knife, he stepped on the accelerator and drove at breakneck speed to the hospital. He helped Tom walk into the emergency room, where the young man was given immediate treatment. Unfortunately, Tom's wounds were too severe, and he died a few days later. According to Brown, police immediately returned to the scene of the murder, but no sign of the killer or Wanda's corpse could be found. Even the pools of blood that had formed on the bridge were gone. Neither Wanda Smithson nor her killer was ever found.

For more than three-quarters of a century, couples brave—or foolish—enough to drive out to Watauga River Bridge for a little privacy have reported encountering a terrifying figure. People who have seen the phantom up close claim that he wears a monk's robe and has a skull for a face. This same menacing presence has been seen under the bridge and near Stony Creek. Some drivers reported that when they drove over the bridge, an invisible presence opened the rear door on the passenger's side and climbed in the back. Some of the drivers swore that after they drove home, they found an impression from the weight of a human being in the backseat. Apparently in Elizabethton, seeking a little time alone with one's girlfriend or boyfriend can be a very risky venture.

The Bewitching Witch

Roan Mountain is awash in history. For many years, the little town was a whistle-stop on the East Tennessee and Western North Carolina Railroad. The narrow-gauge railway carried passengers from Johnson City, Tennessee, to Boone, North Carolina, between 1882 and 1950. The Cloudland Hotel, which was constructed at Roan Mountain in the 1880s by General John Wilder, was at one time the highest-elevation hotel east of the Mississippi River. Luminaries such as Alexander Graham Bell and Thomas Edison were among the hotel's most famous guests. Today the town is known primarily for the Roan Mountain Rhododendron Festival, which is held in early summer. Ghost enthusiasts, however, are attracted to Roan Mountain by the legend of nearby Dark Hollow Cemetery.

Locals say that around the turn of the century, a woman named Delinda lived in Roan Mountain. Although Delinda was not an exceptionally attractive woman, her passionate nature made her a favorite with the men in town, especially the married ones. Desperate to find a reason for their husbands' infidelity, the wives of Roan Mountain attributed the mysterious hold Delinda had over their men to witchcraft. One day, the wives of Delinda's lovers paid her a call at her house. In one version of the story, the local minister encouraged the women to talk to Delinda because some of her boyfriends had contracted a social disease. The women knocked on Delinda's door for several minutes before reaching the conclusion that she was not home. That same day, one of Delinda's lovers, a man named Jankins, died. In one variant of the tale, Jankins's wife had shot him with a rifle on her return from Delinda's house. In another version, Jankins was cleaning his rifle when he shot himself by accident. The townsfolk found it odd that Delinda was not present at Jankins's funeral, because he had always been one of her favorites. Many people assumed that Delinda had fled town to avoid the angry mob that was bound to form after the funeral. One of the mourners recalled later, however, seeing a shadowy figure hovering near the casket after the service. As soon as the pallbearers picked up the casket, they could tell that it was heavier than it should have been.

Residents of Roan Mountain say that Delinda is a restless spirit. Trapped in a cemetery where she did not receive a Christian burial, Delinda's ghost tries to hitch a ride with anyone who can take her someplace where she can find peace. Some people who have driven past Dark Hollow Cemetery claim to have felt a bump in the car, just as if someone had jumped in the backseat. A few drivers said that when they looked in the backseat, they saw the ghostly figure of a woman sitting there. One young woman was driving past Dark Hollow Cemetery with her skeptical husband when suddenly the car began bucking uncontrollably. She compared the behavior of the car to what would have happened if she stepped on the accelerator and the brake at the same time. After the woman and her husband reached their destination, they returned home the same way, and the car again began jerking when they neared the cemetery.

According to some folklorists, the legend of Delinda has possibly become interconnected with the story of a witch who was buried in a grave on nearby Teaberry Road. To keep the woman's spirit down, her grave was filled with cement. People visiting the witch's grave at night report being overcome with a sense of foreboding. Both legends deal with women who were branded as outcasts because of the unnatural influence they had on members of the community. One might say that Delinda's fate is the price some women pay for the bewitching effect they have on the opposite sex.

The House That Faith Built

Old, abandoned houses seem to be the favorite settings for ghost stories. A close second is bizarre-looking houses with odd inhabitants. Such is the case of the Old Stone House in Alcoa.

The house was built by William Andrew Nicholson and his wife, Fair. They began working on the house shortly after moving to Alcoa from Pickens County, Georgia. The sixty-one-year-old carpenter and stone mason started building his house when he had time off from working at the Alcoa plant across the street. Nicholson said he was building a special house that would last forever because he expected to live forever as well. Referring to his fourteen-room, fortresslike house, Nicholson said, "It cannot rust or rot, and if nothing wrecks it, there is no reason why it shouldn't last a million years." After working an eight-hour shift at the plant, Nicholson worked an additional six to eight hours on the house that came to be known as the Millennium House. Nicholson believed that the world would end in 1969 and only 144,000 righteous people would survive, including himself and his wife.

When Nicholson completed his project in December 1946, the end result certainly seemed to be the fulfillment of his dreams. He had hauled three-hundred-pound pink marble stones to the work site in a wheelbarrow. More than four thousand bags of cement were poured over the stacked marble rock. The walls of the two-story house are two to three feet thick, and the stones in the ceiling are three to five feet thick. The roof contains 432 tons of rock and is said to be able to support the weight of several tanks. Nicholson also dug a six-story-deep well that is five feet in diameter.

Nicholson's labor of love became even more difficult after Fair died of cancer in 1950 at age seventy-two. He attributed her death to his belief that her faith wasn't strong enough. Nicholson continued working on his house until 1965, when he took ill and died. The house stood empty until 1971, when it was sold at auction for $3,900. The new owner, Juanita, converted it into apartments. Because the house had such a weird aura about it, it was also used by the Jaycees as a haunted house for Halloween. The Old Stone House was saved from the city's wrecking ball by a firefighter named Dean Fontaine, who purchased the house for $40,000 and spent another $60,000 restoring it.

Many local residents, especially the younger ones, believe that the spirit of William Andrew Nicholson still resides in his unique home. This is not a totally illogical assumption, because Nicholson did, after all, believe that he would live there for a thousand years. The fact that vandals have taken Nicholson's tombstone from his grave at Clark's Grove Cemetery could also explain why some people believe he is still in the house. Passersby say they have seen eerie lights in the yard. Supposedly he still walks around the premises, day and night. The noises people hear at all hours coming from inside the house when no one is there have led them to believe that he is still working on his strange creation.

A woman who visited the Old Stone House back when it was used as a haunted house at Halloween recalled waiting around the entrance for someone to unlock the building. She and her friends had not been standing there for very long when they heard footsteps coming from inside the house. A feeling of dread washed over the girls because they had been told that the building was empty. They breathed a sigh of relief when the man with the keys finally arrived. Just as he stuck his key in the lock, the girls heard what sounded like a door slamming inside the house. The man led the girls around the house as he looked for the source of the noise, but he found nothing out of the ordinary. The woman said that she and her friend remained in the house, but they never strayed from each other's company.

Over the years, the rumor mill has spun yarns that enhanced the mystique of the Old Stone House. People say that Nicholson was a foul-tempered hermit who worked his wife to death and buried her in the basement. The truth is, though, that William and Fair, who married when they were both teenagers, were a very loving couple. Neighbors recall that Nicholson frequently invited children to play in and around his house. He also gave tours of his home to adults, although he refused to discuss religion with anyone. Actually, the facts in the case of William Nicholson are so bizarre that it seems unnecessary to fabricate fantastic tales about his life and "the house that faith built."

North Tennessee

MOST OF NORTH TENNESSEE LIES WITHIN THE HIGHLAND RIM, WHICH IS an elevated plain surrounding the Highland Basin. Underground streams have carved out caves in the eastern part of the region. The primary cash crops in the northern part of the Highland Rim include tobacco, wheat, corn, and berries.

The Bell Witch: America's Greatest Ghost Story

Witches have been a staple of folklore for centuries. Traditionally, witches have usually been women, although some stories make mention of male witches as well. Witches have always been thought of as people who practice magic, and they can be found in tales from different cultures and time periods. For the most part, witch-craft has been defined as those practices that affect a person's body, mind, or property without his or her consent or knowledge. The people who were accused of being witches during the Salem Witch Trials of 1692 were supposedly perpetrating such acts on their neighbors. More than a century later, another high-profile incident of witchcraft surfaced in North Tennessee. Today, however, some experts in the paranormal wonder whether the Bell Witch was a true witch in the classic sense of the word.

John Bell was a farmer who moved to Robertson County in North Tennessee from Halifax County, North Carolina, in 1804. After purchasing 320 acres of rich farmland near the Red River, he built a large cabin for himself and his family. Over the next decade, Bell's family and fortunes grew, and the family became active members of the Red River Baptist Church. Then one day in 1817, Bell had an experience that changed his life forever. In late summer, he was walking along the edge of his cornfield with gun in hand when he spied a strange-looking animal sitting in the middle of a corn row. The creature seemed to have the body of a dog and the head of a rabbit. Bell raised his gun and fired several times, with no discernible effect. Suddenly the beast dematerialized. Bell was shaken by the incident, but by the time he returned home, he forgot to mention it to his family.

That night after dinner, John Bell was enjoying a peaceful evening when he heard the sound of someone—or something—beating against the side of the house. The pounding sounds, which continued for several nights, were accompanied by a number of even more unsettling noises. His children complained of being awakened in the middle of the night by the sounds of rats chewing on their bedposts. They also heard the sounds of someone kicking against the ceiling, knocking over furniture, and dragging chains across the floor. Later on, they began hearing rocks and sticks being dropped on the floor and choking and gulping sounds.

Before long, the entity became violent. Blankets were pulled from children's beds. Something pulled their hair and scratched them in the middle of the night. For some reason, twelve-year-old Betsy Bell was the entity's favorite victim. She was pinched, slapped, bruised, and stuck with pins. As the violent disturbances escalated, Betsy began having convulsions. She also passed out for no apparent reason.

After a few months, the entity began communicating with John Bell. At first, it made only a series of whistling noises. Then it progressed to whispers. Eventually the entity was able to identify itself in a loud, clear voice as the witch Kate Batts. Local folklore has provided a number of reasons for Kate Batts's hatred of John Bell. One legend has it that John Bell fell in love with Kate Batts when he lived in Halifax, North Carolina. They became engaged, but before they could get married, her lifeless corpse was found next to a well

near her home in 1770. Neighbors speculated that Bell had murdered her because the prospect of marrying such an ill-tempered woman was unbearable. In another version of the story, after moving to Tennessee, John Bell locked Kate Batts up in the smokehouse and starved her to death. The most likely reason for Kate's dislike of John Bell can be found in local court records. In 1817, a Robertson County jury found John Bell guilty of usury in a slave deal with Benjamin Batts. Bell's conviction might explain why Kate Batts wanted to persecute John Bell, but it does not explain why she targeted little Betsy.

John Bell tried to keep his "family trouble" secret, but the task proved to be impossible. He confided in the family minister, James Johnson, who tried to exorcise the entity, but to no avail. News of the strange activity in the Bell household spread throughout the region about a year after it started. People began visiting the Bell Farm. They said that the witch, as she was now known, quoted scripture, sang hymns and bawdy drinking songs, and talked to curiosity seekers. She even repeated, word for word, a sermon that she had heard in a local church. Some members of Bell's church spent the night there to record the paranormal activity, but after a few visits, no one from his parish ever wanted to set foot in the Bell house again.

John Bell's most famous visitor was General Andrew Jackson, under whom Bell and his son John Bell Jr. had fought in the Battle of New Orleans. One day, Jackson and a party of men from Nashville made the journey to the Bell House in a large wagon pulled by four draft horses. The group was approaching the farm when one man made a joke about the witch. Suddenly the wagon jerked to a halt. While the driver cracked the whip, his passengers climbed down and inspected the wagon. They did their best to make the wagon move, but with no success. Finally, an exasperated Jackson exclaimed, "It might be the witch!" At that same moment, the men heard a disembodied voice from the trees overhead say, "They can go now, general." After a few seconds, the voice added, "I'll see you all later on tonight."

After arriving at the home of John Bell, the men began making camp in the yard. One of the men, who claimed to be a "witch tamer," pulled a pistol and vowed that he would shoot and kill the witch with a silver bullet. Nothing happened for an hour. Then the witch tamer ordered the witch to appear. Suddenly, he went into convulsions, screaming that he was being beaten and stuck with pins. As he flailed his arms wildly, the man was flung through the door by unseen hands. Almost immediately the men heard a female voice proclaim that she would identify the "other fraud" in Jackson's party the next morning. His curiosity aroused, Jackson wanted to uncover the identity of the "fraud" Kate had spoken of, but his terrified men persuaded him to leave at dawn the following day. Neither Jackson nor his men ever returned to the Bell Farm.

Over time, John Bell's health deteriorated, and he soon became bedridden. One day, his family discovered that one of his bottles of medicine had been replaced by a deadly poison. On December 19, 1820, his sons discovered their father lying in a coma. They rushed to the medicine cabinet to see if he had been poisoned and found a vial of a dark, unknown liquid that was only a third full. The witch announced that she had given John Bell the potion while he was asleep, and he would never regain consciousness. Bell died the next day. One of his sons gave some of the liquid to the family cat, and the little feline died immediately.

Kate was not finished with the family of John Bell, however. Betsy fell in love with a local boy named Joshua Gardner, and they soon became engaged, despite the fact that Kate told Betsy not to marry him. Everywhere the couple went, the witch taunted them. Finally, Betsy could stand Kate's harassment no longer. On Easter Monday, 1821, she broke off her engagement to Joshua Gardner.

In April 1821, Kate told John's widow, Lucy, that she would return to the family's farm in seven years. In February 1828, the spirit fulfilled its promise. Lucy and her sons Richard and Joel began hearing scratching sounds on the exterior weather boards of the house. Objects were moved to other locations. Blankets were pulled from the beds. Lucy and her sons decided not to acknowledge Kate's presence in hopes that she would eventually leave. Within a few days, Kate left the house and moved in with John Jr. She had lengthy conversations with him, discussing such topics as Christianity and the need for a mass spiritual awakening. She also predicted the Civil War, World War I, the Great Depression, and World War II. Kate communicated with John Jr. for three weeks. Then one night, she bade him farewell, but before leaving, she promised to return in 107 years. There is no evidence that she ever returned.

Several theories have been proposed by experts to explain the bizarre occurrences at John Bell's farm. The first theory, proposed by a British psychiatrist named Dr. Maxwell Telling in the 1940s, suggested that the haunting was actually poltergeist activity produced by the Bells' daughter Betsy. Parapsychologists believe that some emotionally troubled adolescent girls, like Betsy, have the ability to manipulate objects in a house through psychokinesis. But psychokinesis does not explain Kate's conversations with Bell, his neighbors, and John Jr. Another theory, proposed by Nandor Fodor, an expert on paranormal phenomena, holds that Betsy was molested by her father and created a "second personality" in the form of a mental force that could move objects. This theory does not explain how Kate was able to affect her environment when Betsy was not present, however. A third theory, from writer and ghost expert Troy Taylor, suggests that after a burial mound on the Bell Farm was destroyed, a portal was created through which came the entity that called itself Kate Batts. As intriguing as this theory is, it is as difficult to prove as it is to disprove.

Will the Bell Witch ever come back? In a way, she has, through the movies *The Bell Witch Haunting* (2004) and *An American Haunting* (2006). The Bell Witch has also received new life through songs, such as Mercyful Fate's "The Bell Witch" (1993) and a four-song EP titled "Living in the Shadows" (1988), which were both inspired by the legend. The story of the Bell Witch is better known now than it has ever been, thanks to the Internet. Who can say what her next incarnation will be?

Queen of the Cumberland

The Smith-Trahern Mansion in Clarksville was built in 1858 in the Greek Revival and Italianate styles by a wealthy tobacco exporter and riverboat captain named Christopher R. Smith. The main house consisted of a grand hall and four large rooms on the first and second floors. A third-story room and stairs led up to the fourth level, known at the time as the widow's walk.

Christopher and his wife enjoyed all the privileges that wealth provides and were part of a small but thriving social scene in Clarksville. But their happiness was cut short not long after they moved to the town. In one version of the tale, Christopher contracted yellow fever on a trip to New Orleans. His body was loaded onto a steamboat to be transported back to Clarksville, but it was lost when the steamboat exploded. In another version, Lucy's husband was drowned in a sailing accident on the Cumberland River. According to yet another account, Lucy was on the widow's walk watching the river for the steamboat her father and her husband were returning on. Suddenly she saw the steamboat's boiler explode, killing the most important men in her life.

All of the variants end the same way. Unable to accept the unavoidable truth that Christopher was dead, Lucy sat by the window, waiting in vain for him to return. She continued gazing out the window until her death in 1905 at the age of seventy-eight. In 1947, Joseph and Margaret Trahern began an extensive restoration of the old mansion. The Smith-Trahern Mansion was placed on the National Register of Historic Places in 1988 and is now a house museum. If one can believe reports from some of the hundreds of visitors who tour the mansion every year, Lucy Smith's lonely vigil has never really ended.

Not surprisingly, Lucy's ghost is usually seen looking through a window toward the river. The apparition of a woman in a nightgown running through the house at midnight has also been sighted. Before the mansion was restored in 1947, teenagers claimed they heard babies crying in the house. After 1947, locals reported seeing the ghost of a man carrying a lantern walking around the outside of the house. In the 1990s, people who spent the night in the Smith-Trahern Mansion with the national president of Extension Homemakers heard the unmistakable sound of people talking. In fact, it sounded as if several conversations were going on simultaneously, like a party. Just prior to this incident, the Night Owls Club was meeting in the front parlor when the women heard a loud, cracking sound. One of the women investigated and discovered that the globe of a lamp had broken. The lamp was still in an upright position.

The strangest visitor to the Smith-Trahern Mansion was a tourist who knew a great deal about the house and the Smith family. When asked how she had come by this information, the woman replied that she was the great-great-granddaughter of Christopher Smith. Without the knowledge of the tour guides, she managed to spend the night in the old mansion. The next morning, police driving by the house saw the woman standing on the veranda in an antebellum gown, waving to passersby. When police entered the house, they found that the woman had filled a room with toys she had taken from a closet. She claimed that this was the nursery for the child she never had.

Granted, some of the paranormal activity in the Smith-Trahern Mansion can be fairly easily explained. Witnesses could have mistaken the peeping of baby pigeons for the crying of babies. After restoration of the house began, a night watchman made hourly rounds around the outside of the house, and gave rise to yet another ghost story, leading some ghost enthusiasts to conclude that Lucy Smith's solitary vigil inside her beautiful mansion is not so lonely anymore.

Haunted Rugby

Tourist brochures for Rugby promote the secluded little town as a "place apart." Anyone who has spent time in Rugby realizes that this assessment is clearly an understatement. Actually, traveling through Rugby is like going back in time. Lining Central Avenue is a cluster of nineteenth-century board-and-batten houses and public buildings, the remnants of a utopian community founded in the 1880s by a group of expatriates from Great Britain. Their leader, Thomas Hughes, is best remembered today as the author of the novel *Tom Brown's School Days*. Eager to escape the class distinctions of Great Britain, the expatriates planned to develop an agricultural community through cooperative enterprise. By 1884, more than three hundred people lived and worked in the seventy Victorian buildings that graced the town they lovingly called the New Jerusalem. The thriving community had its own general stores, schools, newspaper, sawmills, drugstore, and dairy and butcher shop.

By the mid-1880s, Rugby's future was threatened by financial problems, arguments over land titles, harsh winters, a drought, and typhoid fever. Hughes poured more than $75,000 of his own money into his dream colony, but it was not enough. Most of the colonists had left by 1900, but enough people remained to maintain the buildings and care for the lands. Some of the visitors to present-day Rugby claim that some of the original inhabitants are still there.

One calamity that spelled the beginning of the end for Rugby was the burning of the Tabard Inn. The first Tabard Inn was built in

1882. The luxury hotel billed itself as Chaucer's Tabard Inn because the main stairway was said to have a baluster from the Tabard Inn from Chaucer's time period. After the hotel burned in 1884, an even grander Tabard Inn rose in its place. The second manager of the hotel, a Mr. Davis, moved into Room 13 with his new bride because the guests and staff believed it to be an unlucky room. On New Year's Day 1898, the bodies of Davis and his wife were found on the bloodsoaked bed. The doctor who examined the corpses determined that Davis had slashed his wife several times with a straight razor. After ingesting poison, Davis then shot himself in the forehead with a derringer. Friends of Davis's reported that he had flown into a jealous rage the night before, after watching his wife flirt with a young man at a New Year's Eve party. A few years later, when the second Tabard Inn burned to the ground, Room 13 was the last room to burn.

Evidently, the tragic legacy of the Tarbard Inn found a place in the Newbury House, a modest but elegant inn that is thought to be the most haunted house in Rugby. Much of the furniture from Room 13 of the Tabard Inn was moved to the Newbury House. Because spirits are said to attach themselves to objects, some experts in the paranormal say that the ghost of Mr. Davis might have moved with his furniture into the Newbury House. Locals, though, say that the Newbury House is haunted by the ghost of a British immigrant named Charles Oldfield, whom Hughes had sent to Rugby to report on the success of his fledgling community. Oldfield sent word for his wife and son to join him in Rugby, but he died of a heart attack in Newbury House the night before his son was to arrive. Today the spirit of either Mr. Davis or Mr. Oldfield is believed to be responsible for much of the haunted activity at the Newbury House. Guests in Room 2, where Oldfield died, claim to have been awakened in the middle of the night by the figure of a man leaning over the bed, staring at them. This ghost seems to be particularly fond of disturbing female guests. Alarm clocks have been known to ring several times in the middle of the night in this room. In Room 4, disembodied voices have disturbed the rest of visitors. The hallway lights on this floor have turned off and on by themselves as well.

The Thomas Hughes Free Public Library is another haunted building in Rugby. The structure was built in 1882 by Cornelius Onderdouk, who arrived at Rugby with the first group of settlers.

The library still contains the original furnishings and more than seven thousand volumes, some of which were donated by Thomas Hughes. The presence of the head librarian, a perfectionist named Eduard Bertz, is sometimes sensed in the building during twilight hours. In addition, tourists have seen Bertz's dog trying to get out the front door.

A mischievous ghost is said to haunt Kingstone Lisle, the house where Thomas Hughes had planned to retire. Although Hughes never spent much time in Rugby, he did stay in Kingstone Lisle whenever he was in town. A spirit called the Snoring Ghost is a very active presence in this old house. Residents have heard the sound of snoring while eating breakfast or taking their afternoon tea. This ghost also enjoys pulling the covers off freshly made beds.

Many residents believe that the town was saved from oblivion by Brian Staggs, the founding director of Historic Rugby, who died in 1976. Staggs lived in Roslyn, a private residence once owned by Mrs. Jesse Tyson and her family. In the late nineteenth century, Mrs. Tyson's son, Jesse Jr., loved to take joyrides in the family's tally-ho carriage. As the story goes, he was found of loading the carriage with his friends for trips to and from nearby Sedgemoor. Visitors to the house in the twentieth century said they heard the pounding of horses' hooves and the clatter of wagon wheels outside the house while they were sleeping. Some people claim to have seen a phantom carriage pulled by four black horses and driven by a spectral driver bound down High Street, turn around in the circular drive, and ride off into the darkness. Over the years, owners of Roslyn have also seen the apparition of a hawk-nosed woman in an old-fashioned dress sobbing as she walks through the house. In an upstairs bedroom, people have seen the glowing figure of a tall man in a shroud.

Each year, more than fifty thousand visitors from fifteen countries visit Rugby. Today the town is home to approximately eighty-five people and twenty of the original buildings. Many of the historic residences have been restored by their owners. Plans are also under way to rebuild some of the bygone structures, such as the Alexander-Perrigo Boarding House and three-story Tabard Inn. The rebirth of Rugby will not only please historical preservationists, but it should make the town's resident spirits very happy as well.

The Haints of Hurricane Mills

Hurricane Mills is today the twelfth most popular tourist attraction in Tennessee. The town began in the 1810s when an iron furnace was established on the Western Highland Rim. When the iron ran out in the 1850s, a flour mill was built, and agriculture became the primary source of income for the residents of Hurricane Mills.

Hurricane Mills experienced a growth spurt in the second half of the nineteenth century. The Church of Christ meetinghouse and Masonic Lodge was built in 1871, and the town eventually contained a blacksmith shop, general store, stave mill, woolen mill, and county school. A flour mill was built in the 1890s as a replacement for the original. An iron truss bridge was constructed in 1910. In the 1920s, a combination post office and commercial store operated in the little town. Today, more than five hundred thousand people visit Hurricane Mills each year to catch a glimpse of its most famous resident—and maybe have the same sort of paranormal experiences she did when she lived here.

In 1965, Loretta Lynn was well on her way to becoming one of the queens of country-western music. One day, she and her family were driving around Humphreys County looking for a house sixty miles west of Nashville that the real estate agent had promised would be perfect for her family. The moment Loretta laid eyes on the old mansion with the huge white pillars, she fell in love with it. When she and her husband, Moody, informed the real estate agent that they were in love with the house, they were told that the cost included the town of Hurricane Mills as well. Flabbergasted, Loretta and Moody told the agent that they were very interested in buying the house and the surrounding property. To cover the cost of their new acquisition, Loretta took her act on the road while Moody went to work repairing the decaying mansion and outbuildings. When Loretta and her family moved into their new house in 1966, they discovered that they had purchased much more than an old house and an old town.

They had not lived in the house very long when strange things started happening. Soon after moving in, Loretta saw the door to the bedroom of her twin girls, Patsy and Peggy, open and close by itself. Later, she discovered that the girls had seen ladies in Victorian-era dresses walking around their room. Loretta began hearing someone walking up and down the stairs when no one was there. She soon found that the bedroom on the fourth floor was always cold and dead flies collected on the windowsill. No one in her family wanted to spend much time in the "brown room," as it came to be known.

After the family was settled in the home, Loretta felt something cold pass through her body when she was all alone. She had this experience several times over the years, usually when she was alone. Loretta soon discovered that the scariest place in the house was the slave pit, a small cellar with iron bars over the top, located under the front porch. During the antebellum era, unruly slaves were punished by being chained to the wall of the pit. One day in 1983, Loretta and a friend were watching television when they heard someone walking on the front porch. The women turned on the porch light and looked out the front door, but no one was there. They sat back and continued watching their program, when suddenly, they heard the sound of dragging chains. After listening for a few uneasy minutes, they realized that the sound was coming from the slave pit. Before Loretta and her family moved out in 1984, a number of full-bodied apparitions were seen in the house, including the ghosts of a slave, riverboat captain, and Confederate soldier.

Unclear as to why spirits would be haunting their house, Loretta and Moody began researching the history of the old mansion. They found out that the house was built in 1845 by Colonel James T. Anderson, who had planned to grow peanuts on the land. Despite the appearance of the mansion, it was never a plantation house. The metal columns were added by the owners in the 1930s to give the house the look of an antebellum mansion. Colonel Anderson is buried on the property, and an apparition matching his description has been seen many times in the house. Nineteen Civil War soldiers who were killed in a skirmish not far from the house are buried on the property as well. A lady in white who has been seen by many people in the house over the years is thought to be the spirit of Beulah Anderson, who gave birth to a stillborn baby and then died twelve days later.

In 2003, the Travel Channel produced a documentary titled *Loretta Lynn's Haunted Plantation*. Loretta, who hosted the program, discussed many of the haunted experiences she has had in the old house. She explained that she has psychic abilities, which might have made her more sensitive to the spirits in her house. Loretta has also held several séances on the property over the years.

The singer lived in Hurricane Mills from 1966 to 1984. Today, her house is part of the Loretta Lynn Museum and is open to the public. Loretta lives on a nearby property, but she often walks around Hurricane Mills and occasionally works in the gift shop. Unlike many people, who are uncomfortable discussing their encounters with ghosts, Loretta readily discusses the activity in her house with visitors.

Clement Hall's Lady in White

The University of Tennessee at Martin had its birth in the founding of the Hall-Moody Institute in 1900, where courses ranging all the way from the primary grades to the first year of college were offered. As the focus of the institution shifted more toward teacher education, the name was changed to Hall-Moody Normal School; the school later became the Hall-Moody Junior College. After the junior college was consolidated with Union University in Jackson in 1926, the city of Martin and Weakley County raised money through tax bonds to establish the University of Tennessee Junior College on February 10, 1927.

Between 1929 and 1932, a number of buildings were constructed on campus, including a gymnasium, central steam plant, industrial arts building, greenhouse, and the McCombs Center and Sociology Building. Enrollment plummeted during the Great Depression but surged again at the end of World War II. In 1951, the state legislature renamed the junior college the University of Tennessee, Martin Branch. The name was changed again in 1967 to the University of Tennessee at Martin. In the 2000s, the university is meeting the needs of the future with the addition of a graduate program in agricultural operations and a new degree program in public administration. Students say, however, that the past lingers on in the university's oldest dormitory

Clement Hall was built as a women's dormitory in 1957. Like many college dormitories, it is reputed to be haunted. The story goes that many years ago, a female student killed herself on the fourth floor. Since then, many students who were brave enough to live on the fourth floor have reported a great deal of paranormal activity, including the appearance of a lady clothed in white, usually in the community bathroom. Director of housing Earl White says that the story actually began in the 1970s, when a student left an art project in the community bathroom to dry. A student who saw the lifesize figures standing in the shower stall became so frightened that she reported the sighting to the dean of Women's Offices.

This logical explanation for the source of the Clement Hall ghost story does not satisfy those students and administrators who believe they encountered the spirit. In the early 1980s, David Belote, who was assistant director of housing at the time, was rummaging through the attic when he saw something pass very quickly between two boxes. Belote admits that what he saw could have been a cat, bird, or even another human being. But other witnesses find it more difficult to explain what they encountered in the old dormitory. Tomi McCutchen Parish, a professor of communications, says that in 2003, a film crew from Memphis television station WMC-TV traveled to the university to produce a documentary on the hauntings at Clement Hall. She and the director of university relations, Bud Grimes, were on the fourth floor when both of them heard a door slam. At the time, they were the only two people on the floor. In the mid-2000s, twenty-seven men were moved to the fourth floor of the women's dormitory because of a housing shortage. One young man, Tim Edmond, was alone in his dorm room at 1 A.M. when a stack of DVDs that had been placed squarely on a desk inexplicably fell to the floor. Edmond at first thought that mice might have been the culprits, but when he realized that no one had seen any mice on the floor, he ran over to a friend's room and spent the remainder of the night there.

No one has been able to validate the story of the girl who killed herself in Clement Hall, but this fact has done nothing to discourage students from blaming the resident ghost for any incident that they cannot explain rationally. Indeed, the durability of the ghost story might explain why the university has its annual haunted house in Clement Hall, but not on the fourth floor. No one, it seems, wants to antagonize the Lady in White.

The Dramatic Ghost of Austin Peay

Austin Peay State University in Clarksville was founded in 1927 on the former campus of Southwestern Presbyterian College, which had moved to Memphis. Two years later, the state of Tennessee purchased the institution for the purpose of transforming it into a normal school. The school was immediately renamed Austin Peay State Normal School for Rural White Teachers in honor of the former governor who had died in 1927. Eventually the institution's name was changed to Austin Peay State College. In 1939, the college became a four-year institution. Enrollment swelled in the 1940s and 1950s because of the influx of World War II veterans. During this same period, other fields of study besides education were added to the curriculum. The college gained university status in 1917. Austin Peay State University continues to grow today because of the course offerings at nearby Fort Campbell. Thanks to the students who have reported having bizarre experiences, the university's ghost stories continue to grow as well.

According to John Morris Brown on the website *Ghosts & Spirits of Tennessee*, Austin Peay State University is haunted by two ghosts. One of these campus spirits is the ghost of Governor Austin Peay. For years, students and faculty have reported seeing the late governor walking around campus.

The better-known ghost, however, is a female phantom whom the students have christened Margaret. The story goes that Margaret was a drama student who died tragically before she had a chance to act in a school play. Her ghost seems to favor the Trahern Fine Arts Center. Students and faculty have blamed her for causing the elevator to stop and start, banging on the lockers, and calling the names of people who stay up late on the floor. Her ghost has also interrupted play rehearsals in the building. One afternoon in 2002, a group of students was rehearsing a play when suddenly, the lights dimmed three times. The intervals between the dimming lasted no more than a few seconds. At the time, no thunderstorms were reported in the area, and no defects were found in the wiring.

Ghosts often seem to be as much a part of theaters as curtains, ticket booths, and balcony seating. During rehearsals, actors, stage crews, and audiences may have construed phenomena that they attribute to the antics of the ghosts as signs of approval or disapproval. In Margaret's case, she might be expressing an opinion through the disturbances she causes, or maybe she is simply trying to make her presence known.

The Never-Ending Battle of Fort Donelson

The Battle of Fort Donelson, which took place near Dover, is not nearly as famous as the Battles of Shiloh or Gettysburg, but its outcome had a tremendous impact on the Confederacy's ability to win the Civil War. The battle began on February 14, 1862, when Andrew H. Foote's Union gunboats began firing "iron Valentines" at the eleven big guns in the Southern water batteries. By the end of the one-and-a-half-hour exchange of gunfire, Foote's fleet had sustained so much damage that he was forced to order a retreat. Flush with victory, the Confederate troops threw their caps in the air and cheered, confident that they had sent the Yankees back north where they had come from.

The tide of battle turned dramatically the next day, however. Aided by the reinforcements he had been receiving daily, General Ulysses S. Grant extended his right flank in an attempt to surround the Confederates. The Confederate generals—Bushrod Johnson, John Floyd, Simon Bolivar Buckner, and Gideon Pillow—attempted to halt the Union advance by attacking the Union right. Just as Grant's forces seemed to be giving ground, the Confederate troops were ordered to retreat to the trenches. Grant took advantage of the indecisiveness and confusion on the part of the Confederate generals and initiated a counterattack. At day's end, the Union forces were victorious. On February 16, General Buckner, who had been left in charge of Fort Donelson, asked Grant for terms at the Dover Hotel. Grant's reply was simple: "No terms except an unconditional and immediate surrender can be accepted." As a result of the Union's first major victory of the Civil War, the South lost control of southern Kentucky and much of middle and west Tennessee, opening a door to the heart of the Confederacy. According to some witnesses, though, the battle of Fort Donelson is not quite over.

At first glance, Fort Donelson National Battlefield seems to be a very serene, quiet place. Occasionally, though, the stillness is broken by the reports of rifles and cannons. Phantom footsteps have been heard marching across the ramparts. Sometimes people hear residual cheers and rebel yells, apparently left over from the defeat of Union gunboats by Confederate artillery.

Several locations around the battlefield are also believed to be haunted. One of these places is Fort Donelson National Cemetery, which was created on the site of the abandoned Confederate works. The cemetery was officially established as the final resting place for 670 Union soldiers and sailors in 1867. Fourteen of the buried soldiers belonged to the United States Colored Troops. Most of the Union dead had been buried on the battlefield, in nearby towns, and around makeshift hospitals. Some people say that one of these soldiers, Reuben Hammond, still stands guard over his fallen comrades. He seems to be a lonesome spirit, because he tends to walk behind visitors to the cemetery. He has also been seen waving to people leaving the cemetery. The identity of the ghost is known because some tourists reported that he shouted out his name to them as they pulled into the parking lot.

Two antebellum homes in the area are thought to be haunted as well. The nearby Crow Home was used as a hospital during the battle. Guests at the old house, which is now a bed-and-breakfast called Riverfront Plantation Inn, have said they heard soft voices and weeping throughout the building. Paranormal activity has also been reported at the Surrender House, formerly known as the Dover Hotel. Built in 1851, the Surrender House is now a museum. Several years ago, one of the volunteers had a number of uncanny experiences inside the house. One afternoon, she was getting ready to close the house when she saw the full-bodied apparition of a Union soldier, which vanished almost immediately.

Tennessee has many picturesque towns where time seems to stand still. At Dover, however, the psychic residue from its violent past seems to be activated on a fairly regular basis. In fact, one can honestly say that history comes alive at Fort Donelson National Battlefield.

Reelfoot's Bloody Legacy

Reelfoot Lake is Tennessee's only naturally formed lake. In 1811, the New Madrid Earthquake created the four-thousand-acre lake in Northeast Tennessee. The lake's violent birth seems to have left its imprint on the history of the region. Davy Crockett, who hunted in the "land of the shakes," claimed to have killed 108 bears in a single year around the lake. During the Civil War, the Battle of Island No. 10 was fought eight miles north of Tiptonville. Between 1907 and 1909, the families of local residents who had owned land that was flooded by the earthquake in 1811 claimed exclusive rights to the waters above that land, setting off a dispute with a land development company that had purchased parts of the tract. The settlers donned masks to defend their rights in a violent crime spree, culminating in the murder of a land company official. Following the intervention of the Tennessee National Guard, six of these "Night Riders" were found guilty of the crime, although that conviction was later overturned. Many locals believe, however, that the region's bloody legacy has its source not in the violent upheaval of the New Madrid Earthquake, but in the actions of a lovesick Chickasaw Indian chief.

In the late summer of 1811, a clubfooted Indian chief named Kalopin (or Reelfoot, as he came to be known) went in search of a wife among his own people. Because of his disability, none of the Chickasaw maidens consented to his proposal of marriage. In desperation, Kalopin began looking for love in the neighboring Choctaw village. He planned to ask the chief of the Choctaws, Copish, for the hand of his daughter, Laughing Eyes, in marriage. Despite Kalopin's offer of bundles of beaver skins, Copish refused to allow Laughing Eyes to marry him. Kalopin was outraged, and his initial words of protest escalated into threats. Copish immediately ordered a couple Choctaw braves to forcibly expel Kalopin from the village.

On his way back to the Chickasaw village, the humiliated Kalopin concocted a scheme to make Laughing Eyes his bride. But after he went to bed, he had a dream that made him reconsider forcing the Choctaw maiden to marry him against her will. Around midnight, he was awakened by a terrifying vision of violent earth tremors, huge cracks in the earth, and death on a grand scale. The next morning, the medicine man interpreted the dream. He said that if Kalopin went ahead with his plan, death and destruction would ensue.

Ignoring the medicine man's prediction, Kalopin assembled a small band of Chickasaw warriors and headed for the Choctaw village. Under cover of darkness, Kalopin and his band of warriors slipped into the Choctaw village and abducted the chief's daughter. On the trip home, Kalopin envisioned the grand welcome he expected to receive from his people. But he and his warriors had not traveled very far when they felt a low rumbling deep in the bowels of the earth. Suddenly the trembling voices of the Chickasaws were drowned out by a tremendous roar. As the earth shuddered and shook, massive trees tumbled into gaping fissures in the earth. All at once, a towering wall of water came crashing down on Kalopin, his men, and their captive, and they all sank to the bottom of the newly formed Reelfoot Lake. In the eyes of the Choctaws and Chickasaws who survived the New Madrid Earthquake, Kalopin and Laughing Eyes were victims of the Great Spirit, who expressed his displeasure at their union by stamping his great foot.

Outdoorsmen who make the journey to Reelfoot Lake to hunt and fish say that the presence of the Chickasaws and Choctaws who died in the earthquake can still be felt, even after the passing of two centuries. Some people claim to have heard the soft beating of tom-toms echoing through the night. Others swear that they have seen the shadowy form of Kalopin limping swiftly through the forest with his bride in his arms in a futile attempt to escape the fury of the Great Spirit.

Tennessee

THE MOST STRIKING GEOGRAPHIC FEATURE OF SOUTHEAST TENNESSEE IS the Sequatchie Valley. Sometimes referred to as a rift valley, the Sequatchie has steep escarpments leading to a fairly narrow, flat floor. The mountains of the Sequatchie country are part of the Appalachian Plateau. Southeast Tennessee is a very fertile region, a land of apple orchards, cotton, and tobacco. Today alpaca farms are nestled in the fields where cows and horses grazed years ago. Southeast Tennessee is also home to a number of wineries and vineyards. Outsiders often find it difficult to believe that the same region that has produced bluegrass music also makes some very fine vintages

The Mournful Mausoleum

The word *mausoleum* is derived from the name of one of the ancient world's greatest kings. The tomb of Maussollos, built for the Persian satrap of Caria, was one of the Seven Wonders of the Ancient World. To this day, many wealthy and privileged people have tried to preserve the memory of their importance by constructing elaborate stone resting places for themselves. Over the years, a body of folklore focusing on mausoleums has been generated in small towns and metropolitan areas throughout America. One of the most legendary tombs in Tennessee—the Craigmiles family mausoleum—can be found in the small town of Cleveland, the seat of Bradley County.

The tragic history of the Craigmiles family began in 1850, when twenty-five-year-old John Henderson Craigmiles moved from Dalton, Georgia, to Cleveland, Tennessee. John and his brother Pleasant M. Craigmiles set up a mercantile business and began making money right away. Convinced that he could capitalize on the California gold rush of 1849, Craigmiles decided to purchase a fleet of six two-masted ships, which would transport supplies from Panama to California. John's daring business venture paid off handsomely, but he lost his fortune a few years later when the crews of five of his ships mutinied, stealing the crafts and their cargo. Undaunted, John resumed his shipping business with the one vessel he had left and recouped his losses. Not only was his fortune restored, but so was his status in the community.

John's resilience was put to the test once more after he married Adelia Thompson on December 18, 1860. On August 5, 1864, Adelia gave birth to a daughter, Nina, who was to become the source of John's greatest happiness and greatest sorrow.

Even though John had wanted a son, he became utterly devoted to the baby the instant he first gazed into her beautiful eyes. John and Adelia became so protective of their daughter that in 1871, when she expressed her desire to attend school so that she could enjoy the company of other children, they opted to have her tutored privately at home, where she could be safe from outside influences. Ironically, the person who ultimately posed the greatest threat to the little girl was her own grandfather, Dr. Gideon Thompson.

On October 18, 1871, Thompson pulled up in front of the Craigmiles home in a shiny black carriage. Nina, who loved her grandfather dearly, squealed with delight when he offered to take her and her doll Vivienne for a ride. Adelia was filled with a sense of foreboding when she noticed that the gentle mule that usually pulled the carriage had been replaced with a black horse with a white blaze on his face. Reluctantly, Adelia permitted Nina to ride with her grandfather, provided that he not allow her to hold the reins. Dr. Thompson assured his daughter that he and Nina would drive safely, and off they trotted toward downtown Cleveland.

Once her home was out of sight, Nina begged her grandfather to let her drive. Shaking his head, Dr. Thompson reminded her that he had promised her mother that he would not let her take the reins. Like most people, though, he found it difficult to say no to the charming little creature sitting by his side, so he wrapped the reins around his hand and hers. Thrilled to be driving the carriage, Nina urged her grandfather to go faster. When the carriage reached the railroad tracks, Nina and her grandfather were laughing so loudly that they did not hear the train that was rapidly approaching the railroad crossing. At the last minute, Dr. Thompson pulled on the brake, causing the carriage to skid. For some reason, the terrified horse bolted toward the oncoming train. Dr. Thompson was thrown clear, but little Nina was crushed under the cowcatcher.

The tragic events of October 18 changed the lives of the Craigmiles family forever. Two days later, nearly the entire town joined John and Adelia in a memorial service held at St. Alban's Episcopal Church, the same church where Nina had been baptized three years before. Afterward, Reverend George James wrote in St. Alban's historical register that a "thrill of horror" ran through the entire town. Less than two years later, Dr. Thompson died, most likely from the guilt he felt over his granddaughter's death.

Exactly three years after Nina's death, construction of St. Luke's Episcopal Church was completed on October 18, 1874, at the family's expense as a tribute to Nina. As soon as the church was finished, John began work on a mausoleum at the rear in memory of Nina. It was built of two carloads of Carrara marble with walls four feet thick. Nina's shattered body rests in an ornate sarcophagus designed by Italian sculptor Fabia Cotte. The sarcophagus is surrounded by six shelves along the walls on which rest the remains of John and Adelia's infant son, born after Nina's death. She also shares her mausoleum with her father, who contracted blood poisoning after slipping on an icy street in January 1899, and her mother, who was struck and killed by a car in September 1928.

Not long after Nina was interred in the mausoleum, schoolchildren who played in the churchyard on their lunch hour noticed that red streaks were beginning to form on the glistening marble. They also claimed to have heard sobbing coming from inside the mausoleum. People say that the red streaks deepened with the death of each member of Nina's family. Over the years, all attempts to remove the stains, including the replacement of some of the marble slabs, have failed. Some people interpret the red blotches as a sort of curse on the Craigmiles family. Others are certain that the mausoleum is weeping because little Nina never had the opportunity to enjoy the company of other children.

The Legendary Trees of Tennessee Wesleyan

In the American South, vegetation has become inextricably linked to burial sites. Beginning in the nineteenth century, generations of Southerners have converged onto local cemeteries on Decoration Day, during the first week of May, to scrape grass and weeds from graves as a way of demonstrating that they have not forgotten their loved ones. Sometimes, flowers and trees have been planted in cemeteries as memorials to the dear departed. Cedar trees, which are related to the yew and live a very long time, were planted in some graveyards as symbols of eternity. In some of these "folk cemeteries," crape myrtles and gardenias were planted for the same reason. In rare instances, though, trees have been known to grow mysteriously on top of graves. In these cases, colorful legends often provide the explanations. A good example can be found on the campus of Tennessee Wesleyan College near Athens.

The story begins on September 9, 1780, when British General Charles Cornwallis invaded North Carolina. He was followed by Major Patrick Ferguson and a force of one thousand loyalists. Ferguson ordered the patriot leaders to lay down their arms, or he would "lay waste to their country with fire and sword." The major's inflammatory rhetoric infuriated the Appalachian frontiersmen, who decided to bring the battle to Ferguson. In late September, Colonel John Sevier led a group of Overmountain Men from the Tennessee region across the Great Smoky Mountains in hot pursuit of Ferguson, who turned to face the patriots at King's Mountain near the border between North and South Carolina. On October 17, nine hundred frontiersmen attacked King's Mountain at dawn in eight groups of one hundred to two hundred men. The patriots were repelled by several bayonet charges but continued shooting from the base of the mountain. After several hours of fighting, Ferguson was shot off his horse, and the loyalists surrendered. Not only was the victory at King's Mountain a turning point in the Revolutionary

War, but it also ensured that the original number of colonies in the United States of America would be thirteen instead of ten.

According to legend, one of the British soldiers wounded in the Battle of King's Mountain crawled away into the dense forest near present-day Athens to avoid capture by the patriots. He was about to gasp his last breath when a group of Overland Cherokee hunters discovered him lying on the ground. They carried the soldier to their camp, where a beautiful young Indian maiden named Nocatula, who was the daughter of Chief Attakullakulla, nursed him back to health. The couple spent so much time together, staring into each other's eyes, that they fell deeply in love. After the soldier had fully recovered, he and Nocatula asked her father's permission to marry. Attakullakulla was impressed with the man's stamina and readily gave his consent. Following the soldier's marriage to Nocatula, the chief gave him a new name, Connestoga, meaning "oak."

The young couple had enjoyed only a few weeks of wedded bliss when Connestoga announced that he was going to hunt deer with his new Indian brothers. He was stalking a buck through the forest when he was attacked by one of the warriors who had vowed to drive all whites from Cherokee lands. It is also said that he was in love with Nocatula. The warrior stabbed Connestoga in the throat with a long knife and left him in the woods to die. As soon as Nocatula learned of the fate of her husband, she rushed to his side, only to find that he had already passed away. After declaring her undying love for her husband, Nocatula plunged a flint knife into her heart.

When Chief Attakullakulla learned the identity of the murderer, he killed the warrior. Almost immediately, his rage gave way to deep sorrow. The chief laid Connestoga and Nocatula side by side in the same grave. Then he placed an acorn in Connestoga's hand and a hackberry seed in Nocatula's. The seeds germinated, and the trees grew tall and straight.

Eventually Tennessee Wesleyan College was built on the site, and the two trees became a rendezvous spot for lovers. In 1945, the 165-year-old hackberry became diseased and had to be cut down. Five years later, the oak tree died, and it was removed as well. A metal tablet now marks the place where the trees once stood. To this day, the shadowy forms of a man and woman are occasionally seen near the tablet. Some of the more romantically inclined witnesses have even reported overhearing the lilting tones of a female voice saying, "I love you." Legends such as the story of Connestoga and Nocatula endure because they testify to the undying nature of true love.

Read House Hotel's Ghost Room

Like the phoenix of Greek mythology, the Read House Hotel in Chattanooga can be said to have risen from the ashes. The first hotel on this spot was the Old Crutchfield House. According to local lore, Thomas Crutchfield promised the owner of the Western and Atlantic Railroad that if Chattanooga became a whistle-stop on the railroad, he would build a grand hotel to accommodate the passengers. Construction of the hotel began in 1843 and ended in 1847. In 1861, when Jefferson Davis, president of the Confederate States of America, gave a speech about secession at the hotel, Thomas's brother William interrupted Davis's speech and called him a traitor. William's outburst almost provoked a riot, convincing Thomas that he should sell the hotel before war was declared.

During the Civil War, the hotel was used as a Confederate hospital. The Old Crutchfield House survived the devastation brought on by the Civil War, but it was severely damaged by a flood in 1867 and completely destroyed by fire later that same year. Soon thereafter, a new building was constructed on the site of the previous structure. Dr. John Read took possession of the building in 1871 and converted it into a hotel. In 1926, all but the north section of the hotel was demolished and replaced by a ten-story Georgian-style building. The Read House Hotel was extensively renovated in 2004 at the cost of $10 million. The additions of such amenities as Internet access and a new swimming pool were intended to bring the old hotel into the twenty-first century. But according to staff and guests at the hotel, one holdover from the early twentieth century still remains.

Admittedly, the ghosts of the soldiers who died at the Old Crutchfield House could be the ones haunting the Read House Hotel. Still, most people who are familiar with the hotel's history believe that the ghost of a former guest, Annalisa Netherly, makes occasional appearances in Room 311. Some say that Annalisa traveled to Chattanooga from San Francisco with her husband. Others believe that she was a prostitute. At any rate, Annalisa's lover caught her having an amorous interlude with another man in Room 311. In a fit of jealous rage, he cut her throat in the bathtub. The earliest variant of the tale dates back to 1863, when a Union soldier was said to have solicited the services of a local prostitute at the Old Crutchfield House and then murdered her in a dispute over payment. Regardless of which version of the story one accepts, most people agree that the ghost is female and spends most of her time in Room 311.

As a rule, the staff at the Read House Hotel refrains from booking anyone in Room 311 unless no other rooms are available. Over the years, guests have had a variety of paranormal experiences in this room. Most agree that she does not tolerate smoking. In fact, so many guests had their cigarettes put out by an unseen hand that management changed the smoking section of the hotel from the third floor to the fifth. In *Ghosts of the Southern Tennessee Valley*, Georgiana C. Kotarski reports that an employee named Howard Johnson was lying in bed and watching a football game in the late 1990s when he noticed a strange woman standing in the doorway. He asked the woman if he could help her, but she just stood there and said nothing. Howard called the front desk to tell the clerk that a woman on the third floor apparently needed help. But when he looked back at the doorway, she was gone.

In August 2007, a husband and wife who spent the night in Room 311 had an even closer encounter with Annalisa. At 3:30 A.M., the woman was awakened by the sound of something rolling around on the bathroom floor, like a marble. A few minutes after the rolling sound stopped, the bathroom door closed by itself. Undaunted, the couple did not request a different room. The next night, after working on his laptop computer until 3 A.M., the man decided to retire. He was just drifting off to sleep when he heard a clicking sound. Then, out of the corner of his eye, he saw a shadowy figure standing next to the bed. Resisting the temptation to look, he could sense that the face of the apparition was pressed close to his own. Suddenly, the entity vanished as quickly as it had materialized. The man glanced at a different part of the room and observed the murky form move in front of the dresser. After the apparition seemed to be gone for good, he turned to wake up his wife and learned that she too had been awakened by the cloudy shape passing in front of the chest of drawers. He was relieved to find that he had not imagined the entire incident.

Annalisa has made her presence known in other ways as well. Guests staying in Room 311 have heard ghostly knocking at the door. When the door is opened, no one is there. Lights seem to go on by themselves. Mirrors have fallen off the wall for no apparent reason. At the Read House Hotel, guests stay in Room 311 at their own risk.

The Headless Gownsman

The University of the South, commonly known as Sewanee, was founded in 1857 by ten delegates of the Episcopal Church. The cornerstone of the first building was destroyed by Union soldiers. After the war, fragments of the cornerstone were returned to the university, and they have been mounted in a wall of All Saints' Chapel. The university resumed operations in 1866. Originally, it consisted of schools of law, nursing, medicine, and dentistry. Today, only the College of Arts and Sciences and the School of Theology, as well as a graduate program called the School of Letters, remain. The University of the South in many ways appears at first glance to be a remnant of the past. Male students wear coats and ties to class every day, and professors and members of the honor society wear black robes. Apparently there is another robed figure on campus that is part of the university's past.

One of the university's best-known organizations is the Order of the Gownsmen. Students who have earned the highest GPAs are granted membership in the most elite group on campus. Members wield considerable influence at the university and are allowed to vote on issues that affect the entire school. They can be distinguished from the rest of the student population by their long black robes.

The university's signature ghost story has been passed down from upperclassmen to freshmen for many years. The standard version of the tale, which was included in W. K. McNeil's *Ghost Stories from the American South*, was told to Andy Fulkerson in 1974 by a twenty-nine-year-old Episcopal priest named Reese Hutcheson, who received his degree in 1971 from the University of the South. According to Hutcheson, years ago, several theology students were cramming for final examinations. Late into the night, all but one of the students decided to go to bed. The student who wanted the study group to continue began arguing with his friends. A scuffle ensued, and the candle by which the young man was studying went out. When he reached out to find the candle, his head toppled from his neck. The explanation provided by his friends was that he had studied so much that his head literally fell off. Supposedly, the ghost of the Headless Gownsman still floats around the campus, looking for his head.

One of the most repeated stories of the Headless Gownsman concerns a woman named Mrs. Tucker, who was returning late one evening from Forensic Hall when she met a robed figure whom she assumed was a student. She became apprehensive when it became apparent that the student was not going to get out of her way. As the figure brushed past her, she glanced toward its face. To her surprise, she did not see a recognizable face. On reflection, she was not certain that the figure even had a face. The number of eyewitnesses on campus like Mrs. Tucker is dwindling because the Headless Gownsman was last seen in 1988, marching in a procession for the Founder's Day Convocation.

Some folklorists believe that students tell ghost stories as a way of relieving the tedium of academic life. The legend of the Headless Gownsman of the University of the South is more fantastic than most of these tales, probably because it plays upon the exaggerated fear some freshmen have that if they cram too much knowledge into their brains, their heads will explode. The tale probably originated in the mind of a student or faculty member with an oversize sense of humor and an imagination to match.

The Phantom of Suck Creek

Some of the most breathtaking scenery in Tennessee can be found in the mountains that make up the Cumberland Plateau. Visitors stand in awe as they take in the beauty of the region's cliffs, gorges, waterfalls, and curious rock formations. The Tennessee River Gorge, which encompasses twenty-seven thousand acres of land carved through the Cumberland Mountains, is the fourth-largest river canyon east of the Mississippi. The Cumberland Plateau also contains some of the largest stretches of contiguous forest in the eastern United States. A good example is the twenty-six-thousand-acre Prentice Cooper State Forest, which sits atop Suck Creek Mountain.

Suck Creek received its strange name because it creates whirlpools and eddies as it empties into the Tennessee River. On the edges of Prentice Cooper State Forest sits the little community of Suck Creek, a short distance from Chattanooga. One of the hiking trails in the state forest, the Cumberland Trail, is said to be haunted by the spirit of a runaway slave.

Slavery in Tennessee has a long history. Spanish explorer Hernando De Soto probably brought the first enslaved blacks to the area that became Memphis. One hundred years later, the French Army was accompanied by more than twelve hundred blacks and Native Americans to Fort Assumption. Slaves came along with the first settlers from Virginia and North Carolina who began pouring into Tennessee in 1790. By the time Tennessee had become a state on June 1, 1796, 10,613 African Americans were working on plantations and farms in the state. To protect slaves from abusive owners, the legislature passed the Tennessee Slave Code, which guaranteed the slaves food, clothing, shelter, and medical attention. The code also afforded slaves the right to contract for their freedom. Slaves who were unable to work were protected as well.

Unfortunately, not all masters abided by the Tennessee Slave Code. A particularly repulsive case of abuse in Suck Creek has been preserved in stories passed down by both blacks and whites. It is said that a slave whose name is unknown decided to run away rather than endure working in the hot sun and being beaten by a sadistic master and overseer. When no one was watching, he walked away from the farm. Once he reached the woods, he began running down the path that is now known as the Cumberland Trail. He had run about a mile when he heard the baying of his master's bloodhounds in the distance. The man hid in the bushes long enough to catch his breath and then took off again. He ran for another hour, when he passed out from exhaustion and collapsed on the trail.

He was still lying on the trail when his master and several hired hands caught up with him. After beating and kicking the unconscious slave, his pursuers tied a rope around his neck and hauled him up into a nearby tree. They tied off the other end of the rope, then left the slave dangling from an overhanging branch, certain that he was dead. But unknown to his master, the slave was still alive. Somehow he worked the noose off his neck and fell to the ground.

The next morning, the slaveowner and his men returned to the tree where they had lynched the slave and were shocked to find him gone. They did not have to look very long before they found the slave's hiding place. This time, they tied him up, threw him over the back of a horse, and brought him back to the farm. To make sure he did not escape a second time, the slave was beaten, mutilated, and hanged in front of the slave shacks as an object lesson for anyone even thinking of escaping.

Some experts in the paranormal believe that the agony of the tortured slave was so terrible that it is embedded in the rocks, the trees, and the ground itself. At the point where the Cumberland Trail crosses Highway 27, passing motorists have reported seeing the ragged figure of a man as he dashes through the woods and across the highway. At other times, the apparition appears to be wandering aimlessly along the Cumberland Trail. In addition, the cries and moans of the slave have been heard in the vicinity of the hanging tree. People who are familiar with the tale believe that the slave is searching endlessly for his tormentors, none of whom were ever brought to justice.

Southwest Tennessee

SOUTHWEST TENNESSEE ENCOMPASSES THREE PARTS OF THE GULF Coastal Plain. A hilly region runs along the west bank of the Mississippi River. A number of low, rolling hills and wide valleys make up an area called the Bottoms. The third region, the Mississippi Alluvial Plain, is a major producer of cash crops. Southwest Tennessee includes Memphis, the state's largest city and home to many historic and haunted locales.

Graceland's Ghost

Graceland in Memphis has become a shrine to its best-known occupant, Elvis Presley. The property on which the mansion is located originally was part of a 500-acre Hereford cattle farm, established in 1861 by S. E. Toof, publisher of the *Memphis Commercial Appeal*. Toof called his farm Graceland after his daughter Grace. The 13.25-acre plot that eventually became Elvis Presley's estate was given to a niece, Ruth Moore. In 1939, Ruth and her husband, Dr. Thomas Moore, built the Colonial-style mansion that has come to be what is known as Graceland today.

Elvis, who had been living in Memphis in a house on 1034 Audubon Drive, purchased the mansion in 1957. Shortly after moving in, he made a number of changes to the house and grounds, including a wrought-iron "music gate," a fieldstone wall surrounding the property, and the famous Jungle Room, which includes an indoor waterfall. Over the next twenty years, Graceland was home not only for Elvis, but also for his father, Vernon; his mother, Gladys; and his wife-to-be Priscilla Beaulieu, who lived there for five years before she and Elvis were married on May 1, 1967. She continued living in Graceland for another five years, until the couple was separated in 1972. Elvis died in Graceland on August 16, 1977, of a heart attack, most likely brought on by prolonged drug abuse. Elvis, his parents, and his grandmother are buried in another modification he made to the estate: the Meditation Garden.

Since Graceland opened to the public in 1982, thousands of tourists have visited Elvis's home, half expecting to see him in the house that still bears his personal touch. According to firsthand accounts, a few of these people got their wish.

The large number of images of Elvis captured on film by visitors soon after his death fueled speculation that the King was still alive. Not long after his death, a visitor photographed a spectral figure bearing a striking resemblance to Elvis in the pool room. A few years later, a woman claimed to have acquired a photograph in which Elvis can be clearly seen sitting on the living-room sofa. In *Strange Tales of the Dark and Bloody Ground*, Christopher Coleman reports that in 1985, a British tourist photographed what looks like the face of Elvis Presley staring out of a downstairs window. Two years later, a tourist from Missouri left his tour group to shoot a quick picture of the front of the mansion. As the man raised his camera and prepared to shoot, he was shocked to see Elvis staring down from a window on the second floor.

A few people have said that they saw Elvis at Graceland. According to Coleman, one of the first recorded sightings at the mansion involved a woman named Lorraine Hartz, who encountered Elvis as a full-bodied apparition on the grounds. The King also has been observed riding his black horse, Jack, galloping around the grounds. Others have reported that his ghost was hovering around his grave in the Meditation Garden. A woman gazing at one of Elvis's capes in a glass case was shocked to see his disembodied face staring back at her from the glass. Some pilgrims to Graceland even claim to have witnessed a spectral marriage between Elvis and Marilyn

Monroe at the Chapel in the Woods on the Graceland estate. On some dark, misty nights, a ghostly limousine has been seen at the gates of Graceland at 2:30 A.M.

In his online article "The Pilgrimage to Elvis Presley's Graceland," Jim Davidson writes that the majority of the visitors to Graceland whom he interviewed did not report a spiritual interaction. Most of these people admitted, however, that they desired some sort of physical or spiritual encounter with the King of Rock and Roll. The testimony of visitors who have had such an experience suggests that Elvis still enjoys the love and adoration heaped upon him by his legions of fans, for whom Graceland has become the only place where his presence can still be felt.

The Orpheum Theatre's Permanent Occupant

The Orpheum Theatre in Memphis is one of the nation's finest movie palaces from the 1920s. It was built in 1928 on the corner of Main and Beale Streets. The first building on this site was the 1890 Grand Opera House, which promoted itself as the classiest theater outside of New York City. In 1907, the Grand Opera House changed its name to the Orpheum Theatre when it became part of the Orpheum circuit of vaudeville shows. Then, on April 16, 1923, a fire broke out in the fourth-floor "sweatshop" after a performance by a striptease artist named Blossom Seeley. Fortunately, by the time the fire had breached the auditorium and lobby firewall and raced across the auditorium ceiling, most of the audience had left the theater.

Five years later, the Orpheum was rebuilt on the foundation of the Grand Opera House at a cost of $1.6 million. The new Orpheum was twice as large as the Grand Opera House and even more lavishly decorated, with gilded moldings, fifteen-foot, two-thousand-pound chandeliers of hand-cut Czechoslovakian crystal, tasseled brocade draperies, and a Mighty Wurlitzer pipe organ. In 1940, at the end of the vaudeville period, the Orpheum was purchased by the Malco movie theater chain and converted into a first-run movie house. After the Malco chain decided to sell the Orpheum Theatre, plans to demolish the old building and replace it with an office building were reportedly in the works.

In 1977, the Orpheum Theatre was saved from the wrecking ball when it was purchased by the Memphis Development Foundation. After a few months, the newly restored Orpheum Theatre was reopened as a world-class performing arts center. On Christmas Day 1982, it was closed for two years and restored further at a cost of $5 million. The reopening of the theater in 1984 heralded the revitalization of downtown Memphis. The Orpheum has now hosted more Broadway productions than any other theater in the United States. In addition, it has brought to Memphis a wide variety of performers, including Tom Jones, the Vienna Boys Choir, Robert Goulet, Patti LaBelle, Harry Connick Jr., Dorothy Hamill, and Kenny G. But theatergoers and staff say that the Orpheum Theatre's best-known unbilled attraction is the ghost of a little girl.

The details of the story of the Orpheum's ghost vary, depending on who is telling the tale. In 1921, a twelve-year-old girl named Mary was struck and killed by a car on Beale Street. For some reason, her spirit found a new home in the Orpheum Theatre. She seems to be a mischievous ghost who has caused no real harm to people or property. Witnesses have seen doors open and close by themselves. People have also heard the giggling of a little girl and the sound of small feet running up and down the aisles. Some have observed the transparent figure of a young girl roaming around the top aisles of the balcony. Staff members working late at night say they have heard what sounds like untrained hands making tentative efforts to play the organ. Dozens of people who have gotten a good look at Mary describe her as an adolescent girl with brown braided hair, a white dress, and long, black stockings. She is usually seen sitting quietly in her favorite seat, Row C, Seat 5. The most famous eyewitness is Yul Brynner, who saw her ghost in the 1950s while rehearsing for a production of *The King and I*.

Vincent Astor, the building supervisor, organist, and historian, never saw the ghost, but he did report experiencing a strange feeling whenever she was around. One day in 1972, Astor was changing a lightbulb when he sensed that someone was looking over his shoulder. At the same time, he was chilled to the bone. He described the feeling as "getting into a bathtub of cold liver." Over the years,

Astor received many reports from terrified workmen who claimed to have heard the crying of a young girl and the sound of doors slamming after the theater was closed. In 1976, a young member of Ballet South named Anna told him that one night after rehearsals had ended, she walked down to the pay phone in the lower lobby to call her father for a ride home. She did not know where the light switch was, so she had to grope her way through the eerie darkness. After a couple minutes, Anna found the dimly lit phone booth. She called her father, and as she was exiting the phone booth, all the lights on the floor came on. Anna was certain that Mary's ghost had turned on the lights for her.

Astor's most disturbing encounter with Mary took place in 1979, when he was playing the song "Never, Never Land" on the Wurlitzer for a group of visitors. Suddenly one of the young women in the group noticed a little girl with brown hair back in the lobby, dancing to the music. When two other members of the group walked up the aisle toward the lobby, the little ghost disappeared. At that moment, Astor recalled that "Never, Never Land" was reputed to be Mary's favorite song.

Mary's apparition has caused so much commotion at the Orpheum Theatre that attempts have been made to contact her. In 1977, members of the traveling cast of *Fiddler on the Roof* had so many bizarre experiences in the theater that they demanded that a séance be held in the upper balcony. Two years later, a Memphis University parapsychology group investigated the old theater by means of séances and a Ouija board. They learned that the girl had died in a fall that had nothing to do with the Orpheum Theatre.

Tales of ghostly encounters are as integral to the theater's history as old playbills and posters. Mary, the ghost of the Orpheum, may have quickened the pulses of people who have heard her or seen her, but she has never interrupted a single performance at the old theater. Apparently, she adheres to the old adage "The show must go on."

Mystery of the National Ornamental Metal Museum

Situated high on a bluff south of downtown Memphis, the National Ornamental Metal Museum is dedicated to ornamental metalworking in all forms. The museum's forged-steel gates, painted white with gold-leaf trim, sport hundreds of imaginative rosettes. The gates were created by 160 metalsmiths from seventeen countries. The museum opened in 1979 on the site of the old U.S. Marine Hospital, which dated back to the late nineteenth century. The nurses' dormitory was converted into the museum's gallery. The white building, which was built in 1870, was moved to the museum site in the 1930s. Several new buildings were constructed by the Works Progress Administration in the mid-1930s. In 1986, construction of the Schering-Plough Smithy was completed. It features metalworking demonstrations for visitors, classes for area residents, and workshops for metalsmithing students. The smithy also includes a laboratory for metal preservation and conservation. In the foundry, located next to the smithy, steel is melted and poured into molds. The more than three thousand items in the museum include silver jewelry, wrought-iron crucifixes, copper vases, and gothic boxes. Legend has it that the museum's collection also includes a ghost or two.

Staff at the metal museum began having ghostly encounters almost immediately after it opened. One intern living in the dormitory was awakened every night at 3 or 4 A.M. to the sound of bottles and jars being swept off the shelves in the bathroom. Inexplicably, the commotion stopped once the walls were painted. Other interns claim to have seen the ghost of a man in a wheelchair on the second floor of the white building, which served as a center for yellow fever research in the 1870s. Not surprisingly, the most haunted part of the museum is the basement, which originally housed the hospital's morgue. The ghosts of some of the yellow fever victims are believed to be responsible for most of the paranormal activity in the museum.

Most of the evidence that Michael Espanjer, director of the Memphis Paranormal Research Team, has collected has been on the grounds where victims of one of the city's yellow fever epidemics were buried. "We've gotten photographs and cold spots that drop 30 degrees, much more than average cold spots do," Michael says. "We've gotten orbs on the grounds that were three feet in diameter. We tried, but we couldn't explain them away. We captured [on film] the face of a little girl inside one of the drawers in the morgue."

Not everyone associated with the National Ornamental Metal Museum believes it is haunted. Jim Wallace, who has been director of the museum since it first opened, has never seen anything paranormal on the site and believes that all of the ghost stories about the place are ridiculous. On the other hand, the public relations director for the museum, Linda Raiteri, says that anything is possible.

Mournful Molly Woodruff

The Woodruff-Fontaine House is one of the most beautiful mansions in Memphis. A carriage maker named Amos Woodruff built the French Victorian mansion in 1870 at 680 Adams Avenue, in a neighborhood known as Millionaires' Row. In 1883, Woodruff sold his home to Noland Fontaine, a well-to-do cotton factor. Fontaine and his family lived there for forty-six years. After it was sold in 1929, the Woodruff-Fontaine House became a shabby remnant of a more genteel age. The house was extensively renovated and became a house museum in the 1960s. The fine, old home is now a happy place where scores of weddings have taken place since it reopened. Some visitors sense the sadness that still lingers there, however, especially in the second-floor bedroom of Mollie Woodruff.

Even though Mollie Woodruff was born with the proverbial "silver spoon" in her mouth, her life was filled with sorrow. After Mollie and Egbert Woodridge were married on December 18, 1871, she and her husband lived in a suite across the hall from her parents' bedroom. Four years later, Mary experienced the first of a series of tragedies that changed her life forever. Her first child died soon after birth in her bedroom on February 13, 1875. Then in May, Egbert contracted pneumonia on a boating trip. He was brought home to recover, but he died three days later in the same room as his infant son. He was twenty-nine years old. On June 14, 1883,

Mollie married again, this time to James Hennings. The couple lived in the same suite that she and Egbert had occupied. She and James also had a son, but he died at birth on January 13, 1885. Thirty-two years later, Mollie died while visiting her sister's home on Poplar Street.

Staff at the Woodruff-Fontaine House say that Mollie Woodruff is still very much the lady of the house. They say that if she disapproves of the way the furniture is arranged, she expresses her displeasure by slamming doors or breaking objects. One docent reported that she actually heard a spectral voice say, "My bed doesn't belong there." A medium once told the director of the house museum that a spirit that identified itself as Mollie told her that the bed in the Cabbage Room should have been placed next to the staircase wall. Returning the furnishings to their original places is usually enough to pacify the finicky ghost.

In 1980, Mrs. Elizabeth Dow Edwards, the great-granddaughter of Mollie's sister Sarah, said that she and a friend, Margo Ramsey, were cataloguing costumes when Margo's daughter Melissa told them she had felt the presence of someone behind her while she was walking down the stairs. When she turned around, no one was there. One day, Margo heard someone say, "My dear," when she was alone in the house. Jean Crawford, director of the house in the 1990s, said that volunteers have heard a female voice whispering, "Oh dear! Oh dear!" She also heard the sound of a baby crying in the bedroom where Mollie's first child and Egbert died. Once a professor and a tour guide were standing in the Cabbage Room when they witnessed wrinkles on the bed covers being smoothed out by an invisible presence. On another occasion, the apparition of a young woman in a green dress was seen walking back and forth between the bedroom window and the nursery.

Most of the time, the staff enjoys working at the Woodruff-Fontaine House. Once in a while, though, they get the impression that they are sharing the house with Mollie Woodruff, who returns to the site of the happiest and saddest periods in her life. The Woodruff-Fontaine House is still Mollie's home, and apparently she wants no one to forget this fact.

Voodoo Village

For generations of Southern children, visiting haunted places in the dead of night is a rite of passage. In many towns and cities, out-of-the-way places such as cemeteries and bridges are favorite places for high school and college students to drink, talk, and make out. The appeal of these remote areas is enhanced if they happen to be off-limits. One such place is a small neighborhood located in a cul-de-sac of Mary Angela Road in southwest Memphis. This fenced-in compound is known by locals as Voodoo Village.

The existence of Voodoo Village was relegated primarily to legend and rumor until the 1960s, when fights between white and black youths in the area were reported by local newspapers. Since that time, this "dangerous" area has been a favorite haunt of teenagers intent on proving their adulthood or earning admission into secret clubs or gangs. According to one young woman, when she was in high school, she heard stories of a strange neighborhood composed of ramshackle houses where people practiced odd rituals and sacrificed small animals. Her friends claimed that inside the compound was a temple whose walls were covered with crosses, sunbursts, and hearts. The temple contained candles, voodoo dolls, a statue of a thunderbird with horns, and Egyptian masks. The centerpiece of the temple was a statue of Jesus, holding a Bible with a dagger through his hand. It was said that while the rituals were performed, the eyes of Jesus glowed, and blood dripped from the dagger.

Stories circulated by visitors and journalists portrayed Voodoo Village as a very dangerous neighborhood. Most of the time, a gate prevented nonresidents from gaining entrance. It was said that those who were able to drive into Voodoo Village found themselves on a dead-end road so muddy that their car sank up to its door handles, trapping them inside. Those interlopers who were lucky enough to escape the mud traps found that the roads they drove in on were blocked by a school bus that appeared out of nowhere. People unlucky enough to be caught trespassing were never seen again.

Once newspaper articles about Voodoo Village had been published, stories that older residents had been telling for years began to resurface. They spoke of an isolated community made up of a mixed race of African Americans and Native Americans. Voodoo

Village was made up of four houses, they said. Inside the front lawns of these houses were statues and carvings decorated with Arabic and Hebrew symbols. The villagers sacrificed animals to Satan to keep themselves young. At one point, so many goats and dogs were being stolen for sacrifice that a group of vigilantes was created for the protection of pets. The residents of Voodoo Village threw rocks at any outsiders who attempted to take photographs inside the compound because they believed that they will reveal the images of trespassers who have been murdered inside Voodoo Village over the years. It is also said that the photographs will reveal the true age of the inhabitants. The unusually high number of deformities and exotic diseases that can be found in Voodoo Village is the direct result of the African voodoo rituals that are practiced there.

Longtime residents of Memphis claim that Voodoo Village is ruled over by a chief named Wash Harris. Legend has it that Harris called his village St. Peter's Spiritual Temple when he founded it in the 1960s. Despite the rumors that his followers worship the devil, he claims that he is doing the Lord's work. In these stories, Harris is depicted as a very charismatic man who supposedly has superhuman powers. One legend has it that once when he was arrested by the Memphis Police Department, he escaped from his jail cell simply by dematerializing. In a few rare interviews that he gave in the 1980s, Harris took credit for most of the artwork inside the village. Some people say that Harris is over one hundred years old.

Is voodoo really being practiced in this small collection of shotgun houses in southwest Memphis? No one seems to know for sure. But as long as stories of animal sacrifice, bleeding statues, and ageless villagers are circulated in Memphis, young people will still venture out into the night to see if they are really true.

Haints of the Hunt-Phelan House

The Hunt-Phelan House at 533 Beale Street was completed in 1832 by George Wyatt. Known as Memphis's "best-kept secret," this sixteen-room, red brick house was built in the Greek Revival style with several architectural oddities, such as an escape tunnel. After Eli and Julia Driver bought the house in 1850, they did some landscaping and added a kitchen. In addition, the original portico was moved to the side of the house, and a new two-story portico of Ionic columns was added to the front of the house.

During the Civil War, the house was owned by Driver's son-in-law, William Richard Hunt. In 1862, the house became the headquarters of Confederate general Leonidas Polk, who planned the Battle of Corinth, Mississippi, while he was there. The Confederate government showed its gratitude for the Hunt family's support by providing a boxcar for the removal of all their possessions before the fall of Memphis. From June 27 to July 12, 1862, the home became the headquarters of General Ulysses S. Grant, who supposedly planned the siege of Vicksburg in the library. The Western Sanitary Commission used the mansion as a soldiers' home and hospital for Union soldiers between 1863 and 1865. The Freedmen's Bureau housed its teachers there as well. Hundreds of freed slaves learned to read and write at the mansion. The tunnel under the house was an Underground Railroad stop for runaway slaves escaping northward. In 1865, the house was returned to William Richard Hunt by President Andrew Johnson.

In the twentieth century, a geologist named Stephen Rice Phelan acquired the old mansion. The reclusive Phelan preserved the history of the house, but he allowed it to fall into disrepair. Phelan's nephew, Bill Day, inherited the house in the 1990s and embarked on an extensive restoration project. The upkeep of the home proved to be too much, however, and Day was forced to sell the furnishings in 2000 and the house itself in 2001. In 2005, this grand relic of the South was converted into a bed-and-breakfast called the Inn at Hunt Phelan by Memphis businessman Bud Chittom and his partners. The original furnishings are gone, but the Inn at Hunt Phelan retains its connection to the past through its traditional fare, the period decor, and its ghost legend.

Like many antebellum homes in the South, the Hunt-Phelan House is thought to have a ghost. The story goes that during the yellow fever epidemic of 1873, the entire Hunt family fled Memphis. Before they left, Hunt gave a faithful servant, Nathan Wilson, a chest of gold to pay for the maintenance of the house and property. Not long afterward, Nathan was found dead in his room. He had apparently succumbed to yellow fever. The mud on his boots and bed suggested that he had buried the gold shortly before he died. All attempts to locate the buried treasure failed. Some people have said, however, that if you go out at midnight when there is a full moon and stand under the "three sisters"—three trees in the front yard—Nathan will guide you to the spot where he buried the gold. In recent years, this task has been rendered even more difficult by the death and removal of the three trees.

A formal scientific investigation of the Hunt-Phelan House was conducted in 2004 by the Memphis Paranormal Investigations Team. One of the members, who had a very high-powered listening device, heard a female voice say, "Get out!" After removing his headphones, he turned to the lead investigator, Ginger, and asked her if she had just told him to get out. With a quizzical look on her face, she said no. All of a sudden, the young man bolted from the house. He did not come back inside.

The allure of the Inn at Hunt Phelan has undoubtedly been enhanced by the legends that have grown up around it. People who have owned and lived in the old house believe that the garden was planted by Varina Davis when her husband, Jefferson, stayed there. Another venerable legend has it that Chickasaw Indians were drawn into the house when one of the female occupants of the house was playing the piano. But the one legend that continues to stimulate the imagination of guests and staff at the old mansion is the story of the old servant who still guards a buried chest of gold.

Campus Ghosts

The University of Memphis was founded in 1909 under the name West Tennessee State Normal School. The institution opened its doors on September 10, 1912. By the early 1920s, the first men's dormitory and library were built. The college changed its name to West Tennessee State Teachers' College in 1925. In 1941, the institution changed its name again, this time to Memphis State College. The college was given full university status in 1957. The next four decades were a time of radical change for Memphis State. The first black students were admitted in 1959. Doctoral programs were initiated in 1966. Several new buildings were constructed in the 1970s, including a University Center and a twelve-story library. Memphis

State University became the first in Tennessee to gain accreditation for its entire curriculum in 1983. In 1994, it became the University of Memphis. Today the institution has an enrollment of twenty-one thousand students and at least two very scary ghosts.

The most haunted buildings on campus are also the oldest. Built in 1912, Mynders Hall is said to have been named for Elizabeth Mynders, the daughter of the university's first president, Seymour Mynders. Legend has it that when Elizabeth died following her twenty-first birthday, her father was so devastated that he asked the architects to design the dormitory in the shape of an "E" to preserve her memory. Unfortunately, because of the odd design of the building, it has never been air-conditioned. Over the years, Elizabeth has come to be known as a very protective spirit who looks after the women who live there. Nevertheless, some female residents have found Elizabeth to be an intimidating presence. Many students have reported seeing a female apparition floating up and down the hallways, ordering the girls to get out. Students also say that the mirrors in the dormitory are hung in the closets to appease Elizabeth, who apparently dislikes mirrors.

Another very haunted building is Brister Hall, constructed in 1928 and named after John Willard Brister. It served as the main library from 1928 until 1994, when it was converted into a testing center. Brister Hall also houses the Heritage Room, where more than 150 items are on display, including yearbooks, class photos, letter jackets and sweaters, football cleats, and diplomas. One artifact that is not contained in the Heritage Room is the ghost of a young woman who was supposedly raped and murdered in the tower of the library. It is said that because the man was never caught, her restless spirit still roams the hallways in an endless search for her assailant. Unlike the ghost of Elizabeth, this is a woeful apparition whose shrill screams have been known to pierce the stillness of the night. Campus lore has it that on several occasions, campus police working the night shift have been dispatched to Brister Library to check out reports of screams coming from inside the building. The source of the spectral wailing has never been found. A few students and custodians have even seen the poor girl's apparition, but she always disappears when anyone tries to approach her.

The campus ghosts at the University of Memphis have little in common, aside from the fact that they are the spirits of women. Elizabeth was a member of one of the most prominent families in the entire community; on the other hand, the identity of the girl who was raped and murdered remains unknown. Ironically, the memory of each young woman is kept alive by the fact that both of them died before their time.

Ernestine and Hazel's Haunted Jukebox

Some of Memphis's most fascinating buildings can be found in the South Main Historic District. One of the most colorful of these structures is a bar that some people might describe as quaint, atmospheric, and maybe even dilapidated. Ernestine and Hazel's, located at 531 South Main Street, is renowned for its live music and its hamburgers, which are reputed to be the best in the entire world. The bar's clientele includes not only young professionals, but even movie people, such as the cast of the film *21 Grams*. The building itself, which was constructed around the turn of the century, has a very interesting history. Over the years, the first floor has housed a dry-goods store and an apothecary. Abraham Plough, founder of the Schering-Plough Corporation, is said to have sold St. Joseph's aspirin and other pharmaceuticals and hair-care products from the building. From the 1920s to the 1950s, the upper story housed a brothel. Today the biggest thrill customers are likely to experience at Ernestine and Hazel's, aside from the ambience and the hamburgers, is its ghosts.

More than a hundred people have experienced the bar's haunted jukebox. Owner Russell George says that once in a while, the jukebox turns on by itself, and the song it plays is always relevant to the conversations that patrons are having at the time. Michael Espanjer, director of Memphis Paranormal Investigations Team, says that one day, he and the owner were sitting in the bar talking about the movie *The Exorcist* when the jukebox began playing the Rolling Stones song "Sympathy for the Devil." "It happens too often to be coincidence. You can almost test it. You can go up to it and say, 'I'm going to talk about hookers,' and a Hank Williams song containing the line 'I laid my money down, and she gave me a good time' will come on," Michael says. George denies rigging the juke-box to turn on by itself: "They said, 'You've got some kind of control back there.' I said we don't have proper electricity to run the place, much less a control."

Michael's group has conducted many investigations at the bar since 2003. "The owner will give us the keys, and we'll spend the night there and let ourselves out the next morning," Michael says. During one particular investigation, a member of the group had a very startling personal experience in the brothel part of the bar. "He was walking upstairs with a friend, and as soon as he put his hand on the stair rail, a cold, clammy hand touched his hand, and it really scared him bad. He was so scared that he lost control of his bodily functions." The most spectacular piece of evidence that the group has collected at the site is a VHS videotape of a full-bodied apparition. "It's eight seconds of incredible spookiness," Michael says. Apparently, more than just good food and drink can be had at Ernestine and Hazel's.

Brewing Up Spirits

In 1877, German immigrants John W. Schorr and Casper Koehler founded a brewery in Memphis. Several of their brewmasters had come from a long line of brewing families. In fact, the family of one brewmaster had been brewing beer for five hundred years. In 1890, the company moved into a castlelike structure at 495 Tennessee Street that became known as the Tennessee Brewery. For more than six decades, the Tennessee Brewery brewed Goldcrest 51 beer and several other labels, until it ceased operations in 1954. Since then, the brewery has stood vacant for more than fifty years, awaiting the new lease on life that has been afforded other historic buildings in Memphis. According to local ghost hunters, though, "vacant" might not be a totally accurate adjective to apply to the Tennessee Brewery.

Memphis Paranormal Investigations Team has investigated the Tennessee Brewery many times. It does not hurt that the director, Michael Espanjer, is friends with the owner. "The Tennessee Brewery is the most haunted place in Memphis," Michael says. "We have tons of photos and video. Unfortunately, I can't put the video on our website because we use a VHS video camera." The group has photographed orbs in motion, energy rods, ectoplasm, odd reflections in a metal mirror, and EVPs. Like Ernestine and Hazel's, the Tennessee Brewery has a haunted staircase. "One time, we were walking up the stairs, and I told everyone to freeze, and we heard footsteps walking behind us," Michael says. He is fairly certain that the ghost is the spirit of one of the German brewmasters who founded the company in the nineteenth century.

Despite the damage incurred by the ravages of time, the Tennessee Brewery is still a visual wonder, with its four-foot-thick walls and elaborate wrought-iron railings and staircases. As of this writing, the fate of the Tennessee Brewery was still unresolved. Plans to convert the old brewery into a condominium and commercial development fell through in 2006. Regardless of what happens to the old building, the fact that it has been placed on the National Register of Historic Places should help preserve its historical integrity. Meanwhile, paranormal investigators like Memphis Paranormal Investigations Team are doing their best to study and document the unusual activity while the building still remains.

Shiloh's Spectral Soldiers

Following the Union victories at Fort Henry and Fort Donelson in February 1862, Major General Ulysses S. Grant began moving up the Tennessee River with about forty-five thousand men. At about the same time, Major General Don Carlos Buell's army of twenty-five thousand Federals was marching down from Nashville. In early April, Grant arrived just ahead of Buell at a small riverboat landing called Pittsburg Landing, just a few miles from a country meeting-house known as Shiloh Church. To keep morale high among his soldiers, Grant decided against having his men dig trenches. Instead, they rested in the woods.

On April 6, a Confederate attack led by General Albert Sidney Johnston came as a tactical surprise. Grant ordered his men, most of whom had never been in battle before, to hold "at all hazards" while he tried to build a defensive line. Brigadier General Stephen Hurlbut's 4th Division made a stand at a small grove of blooming peach trees. Bullets clipped the blossoms, and the bodies of Union

defenders littered the peach orchard, but Hurlbut's men withstood the Confederate assaults for almost seven hours before finally being driven out of the northern end of the orchard. Meanwhile, General Benjamin M. Prentiss took a position at a sunken road that came to be known as the Hornet's Nest. By the time Prentiss finally surrendered nearly six hours later, only twenty-two hundred men—half of his original force—were still alive. By the end of the day, most of Grant's troops had fallen back to Pittsburg Landing, where they were protected by artillery and two gunships. On the second day, the outnumbered Confederates were forced to fall back in midafternoon. When the shooting finally ceased, the Union had lost thirteen thousand men, the Confederates ten thousand. Some tourists, reenactors, and park rangers believe that the Battle of Shiloh is still being fought by soldiers who refuse to stay dead.

Most of the rangers at Shiloh National Military Park will not admit that any paranormal activity takes place in the park. Nevertheless, the park's official position on ghosts has not stopped the circulation of ghost stories among park staff and tourists. Every year, visitors tell rangers that they hear the sounds of gunfire and marching feet when no Civil War reenactors are present. One of the most persistent tales concerns the ghostly drummer boy of Shiloh. In *Strange Tales of the Dark and Bloody Ground*, Christopher Coleman tells the tale of a drummer boy attached to General Buell's army. On the second day of the battle, the boy was ordered to sound "attack" on his drum. The Union soldiers' advance up a hillside was stalled by withering fire from Confederate forces positioned at the top. Convinced that the hill could not be taken, the commanding officer ordered the drummer boy to play "retreat." Instead, the drummer boy played "attack." When the commanding officer asked the boy why he played "attack," the boy replied, "Because it is the only tune I know." Spurred on by the stirring beats of the drum, the Union troops forged ahead and eventually captured the hill. The commanding officer wanted to thank the drummer boy for saving the day, but the boy was dead, shot through the heart.

For many years, this story was considered to be apocryphal. It gained a little more credence in 1940, however, when the skeleton of a boy was discovered during the excavation of a road. The boy had been shot through the chest, and pieces of a drum cord were draped from his neck.

According to rangers and tourists, specific parts of the battle-field are haunted. At Bloody Pond, hundreds of severely wounded soldiers dragged themselves to get a drink. Many of them drowned because they were too exhausted to raise their heads out of the water. So many soldiers died there that the water turned red. Some visitors claim that it still does, although the red tinge in the water might be caused by the rays of the sun. The spirit of a tattered soldier is occasionally seen standing in the ravine between Water Oaks Pond and Crescent Field. Visitors standing by the largest burial mound, where approximately 250 Confederate soldiers are buried, have heard a bone-chilling scream, which park rangers have identified as the rebel yell. Witnesses swear that what they heard was not the hooting of an owl. Several years ago, military historian Jeffrey Gentsch was walking through the woods late one afternoon, when a ranger was telling a group of Boy Scouts the story of the rebel yell. In an attempt to add a little verisimilitude to the ranger's story, Gentsch screamed as loudly as he could. Immediately, the terrified Boy Scouts scattered through the park.

In *Spirits of the Civil War*, Troy Taylor tells the story of a relic hunter who made nightly forays to the battlefield with a metal detector. The park rangers knew that he was digging up unmarked graves, but they were unable to catch him in the act. One night, while some rangers were patrolling the battlefield, they found pieces of a broken metal detector. Not far away was the relic hunter they had been searching for. He was lying on the ground, unable to move or speak. The rangers helped the man to his feet and took him to the hospital, where he was treated for shock. After the man recovered, he refused to explain what had happened to him. Before long, the rumor spread that the man had just exhumed a corpse and was trying to steal buttons from the ragged remains of the uniform when a skeletal hand snatched away the man's ill-gotten treasure. Apparently, park rangers are sincere when they tell visitors that anything that is found on the battlefield stays on the battlefield.

Civil War Apparitions at Cherry Mansion

In 1821, James Rudd set down roots in a well-located spot that was to become Savannah, Tennessee. After building a house on the riverbank, Rudd established a ferry, giving the fledgling settlement its original name, Rudd's Ferry. In 1830, David Robinson took over the ferry and replaced the original house with a brand new structure. A few years later, Robinson presented the house as a wedding gift to his daughter and son-in-law, William H. Cherry. Cherry soon set about to enlarge and improve what came to be known as Cherry Mansion. Around 1880, Alex Haley Sr. arrived at Savannah and became the ferryman of Savannah Landing, located near Cherry Mansion. Haley's wife, named Queen, worked as a house servant for the Cherry family. Their grandson Alex Haley immortalized his grandparents and Cherry Mansion in his book *Queen*. The mansion is also known for the role it played in the Battle of Shiloh and for its paranormal activity.

In 1862, Savannah was a shipping center for cross ties and freight. Its reputation as a center of wealth and culture was soon eclipsed, however, by the horrendous battle that began on Sunday, April 6, near Shiloh Methodist Church. That morning, Union general Ulysses S. Grant was eating breakfast ten miles away at Cherry Mansion. Legend has it that Grant was nursing a hangover from a night of heavy drinking. Even though Cherry was a slaveowner, he was also a Union sympathizer, and he welcomed General Grant and his staff in his beautiful home. At the time, Grant's Army of Tennessee was camped several miles south on the opposite bank of the river around Pittsburg Landing, waiting for General Buell's army to arrive from Nashville. As General Grant was about to take a sip of his first cup of coffee of the morning, he heard the unmistakable roar of cannon fire a few miles away. Setting the cup down, Grant announced, "Gentlemen, the ball is in motion. Let's be off." After sending word to General Buell to march to a point opposite Pittsburg Landing, Grant boarded the steamer *Tigress* and hurried to the battlefield.

After the Civil War, rumors were bandied about that Cherry Mansion was haunted. Residents of the mansion said they experienced frequent poltergeist activity in the old house, such as loud noises and disembodied voices. Full-bodied apparitions have been seen in the house as well. People walking and driving past the mansion have seen a shadowy figure staring out of an upstairs window. All eyewitnesses agree that the man is dressed in a Civil War-era uniform. On his website *Ghosts & Spirits of Tennessee*, John Norris Brown reports that in 1976, four people saw a man in a white suit walk down the street toward Cherry Mansion. When he reached the historical marker in front of the mansion, he disappeared. The identity of the ghost that haunts Cherry Mansion is unknown, although some people have speculated that it could be the spirit of one of two Union generals who died there: W. H. L. Wallace and C. F. Smith.

Today Cherry Mansion is a private residence. The building is not open to the public, but visitors are permitted to walk the grounds and take photographs. The mere fact that the general public does not have access to the inside of the mansion has undoubtedly enhanced the aura of mystery that envelops the old house and perpetuated the old stories that locals still tell about the ghosts.

Hope Hill Cemetery's Dollhouse

Most people would agree that there is nothing sadder than the death of a child. In the nineteenth century, stone masons working in the American South added distinctive touches to the graves of children. Some parents requested that the stone likeness of a lamb or cherub be placed on top of the tombstone. Others preferred that a scalloped stone border called a grave cradle be placed around the grave. To this day, one can find toys and ceramic animals sitting on top of a child's grave. But in a small graveyard located just outside Medina in Gibson County, one can find an even more bizarre memorial to a dead child.

As so often happens in cases where the facts are sketchy, folklore has filled the gaps in the story behind the dollhouse of Hope Hill Cemetery. In June 1931, a five-year-old girl named Dorothy Marie Harvey died and was buried in the cemetery. Some people say that she was raped and beaten to death by her uncle. Others claim that she was the daughter of a family that was on their way to find employment in the North, and before passing through Medina, the child contracted measles and died. Because the family was short on funds, some generous people in Medina chipped in to purchase a fitting tombstone for the little girl. Later, after the child's parents had found work and were financially stable, they had a dollhouse built over little Dorothy's grave because she loved dolls.

As stories of the strange grave shelter spread throughout Tennessee, souvenir hunters and vandals began stealing pieces of the dollhouse. Within a year of its construction, the dollhouse was gone, so the family had it rebuilt. Over the years, the dollhouse of Hope Hill Cemetery has been destroyed and rebuilt several times.

Not surprisingly, the temptation to peer inside the windows of the dollhouse can be too much for people to resist. Some witnesses claimed to have seen Dorothy's ghost playing with her dolls inside the dollhouse. One visitor to the cemetery said that when she was in high school, she and some of her friends went out to Hope Hill Cemetery late one August night to see if the stories were true. They were walking toward the dollhouse when they saw a small, white light just outside the house. The girls stopped for a moment to stare at the light and then continued walking, despite their mounting fear. When the girls looked inside, they noticed an old-fashioned rag doll standing up against one of the walls of the dollhouse. Suddenly the doll fell on its face and turned over. Screaming, the girls ran back to their car and left the cemetery as fast as they could go.

Another young woman said that one weekend, she and a friend ventured out to Hope Hill Cemetery on their own. An elderly man who told them he was a caretaker ordered the girls to leave, even though they were there when the cemetery was supposed to be open. While they were driving home, the girls' resentment at being kicked out of the cemetery grew. After driving a couple miles, they turned the car around and headed back to the cemetery. The man was nowhere in sight, so they walked up to the dollhouse and took a few photographs. After the film was developed, the girls were shocked to see the figure of a little girl staring into the camera.

The tragic tale of Dorothy Marie Harvey has touched the heartstrings of the residents of Gibson County. Visitors have placed flowers on her grave site. Children have left behind toys and crayon drawings. It is certain that as long as her dollhouse remains, Dorothy will never really be forgotten.

Magnolia Manor's Manifestations

Like many antebellum homes in Tennessee, the history of Magnolia Manor is indelibly linked to the Civil War. The Georgian Colonial mansion was built in 1849 by Judge Austin Miller, who is credited with helping plan the southern boundaries of the state so that Memphis was located in Tennessee instead of Mississippi. Constructed of sun-dried bricks handmade by slaves on the house site, Magnolia Manor has walls fourteen inches thick from the ground to the roof.

In 1862, the Union Army used Magnolia Manor as the headquarters for four generals: Logan, McPherson, Sherman, and Grant. The story goes that the generals planned the Battle of Shiloh from the double parlors in the house. For more than a century, members of the Miller family have passed down the story of a rude remark General Sherman made to Mrs. Miller, who was described as a delicate woman. Supposedly, he told her that all Southern men, women, and children should be exterminated. Outraged, she complained to General Grant, who forced Sherman to apologize. Unaccustomed to eating humble pie, Sherman apologized, walked over to the staircase, and slashed the banister with his sword. The scarred banister can still be seen to this day.

Magnolia Manor remained in the Miller family until the 1970s, when the house was willed to the city of Bolivar. In the late 1970s, a lawyer bought the house for his daughter; it was sold to Elaine Cox in 1981. She restored the old house to its original nineteenth-century grandeur and converted it into a bed-and-breakfast in 1995. Today this award-winning bed and breakfast is known far and wide for its Southern hospitality—and its paranormal activity.

Since 1995, a number of guests at Magnolia Manor Bed and Breakfast have had strange experiences. Lights go on and off at all hours. Heavy footsteps have been heard walking up and down the stairs and in an upstairs bedroom when no one was present. A few guests have actually observed a female spirit in their rooms. In the C. A. Miller Suite, guests have seen an elderly woman sitting in a rocking chair just before dawn. One guest sitting in the den witnessed a ghost floating across the room for a few seconds before dematerializing. Elaine Cox says that a few years ago, a guest was lying in bed when he saw the ghost of a woman standing at his door for a few seconds. She then walked over to where he lay and pulled on his shirtsleeve. As soon as the apparition disappeared, the man bolted from the room, leaving his bags inside.

In the 1849 Room, guests claim that a woman in a Victorian dress pulled off their covers in the middle of the night. Some people believe that the culprit is the ghost of Priscilla McNeal, a wealthy cousin of the Miller family who died when she was eighteen years old. Several years ago, a woman who was socializing downstairs during a Christmas party returned to her room to check on her husband, who had gone to bed early. He was not lying in bed, so she looked through the room and was surprised to find him hiding in the closet. He told her that he fled to the closet after something pulled the covers off his bed.

So many sightings have been reported in Magnolia Manor that a local paranormal research group, Mid-South Ghost Hunters, presents ghost-hunting workshops at the bed-and-breakfast. The workshop includes discussion of paranormal investigation theories and methods, as well as an actual investigation of the bed-and-breakfast. During one of the workshops held in March 2006, several members of the group saw a ghost resembling Austin Miller's wife floating past the parlor door. At first the members thought it was Elaine Cox dressed up in a hoop skirt. On close examination, however, they realized that the figure was glowing and transparent. They found out later that Mrs. Cox was wearing blue jeans and working in the kitchen.

In the July 12, 2007, edition of the *Memphis Flyer*, reporter Bianca Phillips covered one of the group's workshops. A participant in the workshop told Phillips that she was checking in during the afternoon when she saw a short, heavyset woman in her sixties with short hair walking down the hallway. The woman was wearing an apron over her dress. The ghost-hunting team told her that she probably saw the ghost of the last family resident of Magnolia Manor, Annie Miller, who died in 1979 at the age of eighty-four. While Phillips was there, one of the participants told her that at approximately 2 A.M., he was lying in bed when a spot at the end of the mattress was depressed, as if someone were sitting there. At 3:26 A.M., Phillips was staring into the open hallway door when she saw what appeared to be a shadow walk across the opening on its way down the hallway.

Before the group retired for the night, the members went to three bedrooms and placed a penny right on top of a photocopy of the coin to test the rumor that the resident ghost enjoyed moving objects. The next morning, the members discovered that one of the pennies appeared to have been moved a little to the right of its copy. While a few millimeters difference is not definitive proof of paranormal activity, it did make everyone present that night wonder.

Bibliography

Books

Brown, Alan. *Haunted Places in the American South*. Jackson: University Press of Mississippi, 2002.

———. *Stories from the Haunted South*. Jackson: University Press of Mississippi, 2004.

Coleman, Christopher K. *Dixie Spirits*. Nashville: Cumberland House, 2002.

———. *Ghosts and Haunts of the Civil War*. Nashville: Rutledge Hill Press, 1999.

———. *Strange Tales of the Dark and Bloody Ground*. Nashville: Rutledge Hill Press, 1998.

Ewing, James. *It Happened in Tennessee*. Nashville: Rutledge Hill Press, 1986.

Flato, Charles. *The Golden Book of the Civil War*. New York: Golden Press, 1961.

Guiley, Rosemary. *Encyclopedia of Ghosts and Spirits*. New York: Checkmark Books, 2007.

Kotarski, Georgiana C. *Ghosts of the Southern Tennessee Valley*. Winston-Salem, NC: John H. Blair Publisher, 2006.

McNeil, W. K. *Ghost Stories from the American South*. New York: Random House, 1985.

Mead, Robin. *Haunted Hotels*. Nashville: Rutledge Hill Press, 1995.

Mott, A. S. *Ghost Stories of Tennessee*. Auburn, WA: Lone Pine Publishing International, 2005.

Price, Charles Edwin. *Haints, Witches, and Boogers; Tales from Upper East Tennessee*. Winston-Salem, NC: John F. Blair, Publisher, 1992.

———. *Haunted Tennessee*. Johnson City, TN: Overmountain Press, 1995.

———. *The Infamous Bell Witch of Tennessee*. Johnson City, TN: Overmountain Press, 1994.

———. *More Haunted Tennessee*. Johnson City, TN: Overmountain Press, 1999.

Roth, Dave, ed. *Blue & Gray Magazine's Guide to Haunted Places of the Civil War*. Columbus, OH: Blue & Gray Enterprises, 1996.

Russell, Randy, and Janet Barnett. *The Granny Curse*. Winston-Salem, NC: John F. Blair Publisher, 1999.

Taylor, Troy. *Season of the Witch*. Alton, IL: Whitechapel Press, 1999.

———. *Spirits of the Civil War*. Alton, IL: Whitechapel Press, 1999.

Turnage, Sheila. *Haunted Inns of the Southeast*. Winston-Salem, NC: John F. Blair Publisher, 2001.

Uchtman, William C. *Volunteer Ghosts: A Directory of Ghosts in Tennessee*. Frederick, MD: PublishAmerica, 2007.

Windham, Kathryn Tucker. *13 Tennessee Ghosts and Jeffrey*. Tuscaloosa, AL: University of Alabama Press, 1977.

Online Sources

"Abe Plough." *The Society of Entrepreneurs*. Retrieved 30 January 2008. http://www.societyofentrepreneurs.com/projects/plough.asp.

"Abe Plough: 1892—1984." *The Tennessee Encyclopedia of History and Culture*. Retrieved 30 January 2008. http://tennesseeencyclopedia.net/imagegallery.php?EntryID = PO33.

"African Ancestry in Tennessee." *AfriGeneas African American Genealogy-Tennessee*. Retrieved 30 January 2008. http://www.afrigeneas.com/states/tn/.

"Are There Ghosts at Falcon Rest?" *Falconrest.com*. Retrieved 4 February 2008. http://www.falconrest.com

"Austin Peay State University." *Wikipedia*. Retrieved 10 February 2008. http://en.wikipedia.org/wiki/Austin_Peay_State_University.

"Baker-Peters Jazz Club." *Baker Peters Jazz Club*. Retrieved 9 January 2008. http://www.bakerpetersjazzclub.com/Bphistory.htm.

Barry, David. "The Dollhouse Grave." *The Ghost Files*. Retrieved 4 January 2008. http://www.ghostvillage.com/encounters/2006/05242006.shtml.

"Battle of King's Mountain." *Wikipedia*. Retrieved 29 December 2007. http://en.wikipedia.org/wiki/Battle_of_Kings_Mountain.

Beck, Ken. "Rugby's Future Depends on Its Historic Past." *TennesseanTravel.com*. Retrieved 3 February 2008. http://tennessean.com/apps/pbcs.dll /article?AID = /20071128/TENNESSEANTRAVEL/3112 . . .

"Bell Witch." *Wikipedia*. Retrieved 24 January 2008. http://en.wikipedia.org/wiki/The-Bell-Witch.

"The Bell Witch." *Studies of the Paranormal*. Retrieved 24 January 2008. http://www.studiesoftheparanormal.com/bellwitch.html.

Boyle, Hal. "Millennium Manor Castle." *Blountweb.com*. Retrieved 22 January 2008. http://www.blountweb.com/millenniummanor/newsarticles.htm.

Brown, John Norris. "Cherry Mansion." *Ghosts & Spirits of Tennessee*. Retrieved 2 January 2008. http://johnnorrisbrown.com/ paranormal-tn/cherry/index.htm.

———. "Haunted Hope Hill Cemetery." *Ghosts & Spirits of Tennessee*. Retrieved 4 January 2008. http://johnnorrisbrown.com/paranormal-tn/hope-hill/index.htm.

———. "The Haunted Read House." *Ghosts & Spirits of Tennessee*. Retrieved 5 January 2008. http://johnnorrisbrown.com/paranormal-tn/read-house/index.htm.

———. "The Haunting of Old Stone House." *Ghosts & Spirits of Tennessee*. Retrieved 4 January 2008. http://johnnorrisbrown.com/paranormal-tn/old-stone-house/index.htm.

———. "The Legend of the Wampus Cat." *Ghost & Spirits of Tennessee*. Retrieved 4 January 2008. http://johnnorisbrown.com/paranormal-tn/wampus-cat/.

———. "Opryland & Music Row Hauntings." *Ghosts & Spirits of Tennessee*. Retrieved 30 December 2007. http://johnnorrisbrown.com/paranormal-tn/opry-row/index.htm.

Bibliography

———. "Rotherwood Mansion." *Ghosts & Spirits of Tennessee*. Retrieved 31 December 2007. http://johnnorrisbrown.com/paranormal-tn/rotherwood/index.htm.

———. "Sighting at Rotherwood Mansion." *Ghosts & Spirits of Tennessee*. Retrieved 31 December 2007. http://johnnorrisbrown.com/paranormal-tn/blog/2005/05/sighting-at-rotherwood-mansion.html.

———. "Sensabaugh Tunnel." *Ghosts & Spirits of Tennessee*. Retrieved 20 January 2008. http://johnnorrisbrown.com/paranormal-tn/blog/2005/04/sensabaugh-tunnel.html.

———. "The Spirits of Austin Peay." *Ghosts & Spirits of Tennessee*. Retrieved 10 February 2008. http://johnnorrisbrown.com/paranormal-tn/apsu/index.htm.

———. "The Spirits of Shiloh." *Ghosts & Spirits of Tennessee*. Retrieved 2 January 2008. http://www.johnnorrisbrown_com/paranormal-tn/shiloh/index.htm.

———. "The Suck Creek Spirit." *Ghosts & Spirits of Tennessee*. Retrieved 30 January 2008. http://johnnorrisbrown.com/paranormal-tn/suck-creek/index.htm.

———. "Wampus Cat Sighting in Knoxville." *Ghosts & Spirits of Tennessee*. Retrieved 4 January 2008. http://johnnorrisbrown.com/paranormal-tn/blog/2005/10/wampus-cat-sighting-in-knoxville.html.

———. "Watauga River Bridge." *Ghosts & Spirits of Tennessee*. Retrieved 12 February 2008. http://johnnorrisbrown.com/paranormal-tn/watauga-bridge/index.htm.

———. "The White Screamer of White Bluff." *Ghosts & Spirits of Tennessee*. Retrieved 3 January 2008. http://johnnorrisbrown.com/paranormal-n/screamer/index.htm.

———. "Woodruff-Fontaine House." *Ghosts & Spirits of Tennessee*. Retrieved 5 January 2008. http://johnnorrisbrown.com/paranormal-tn/woodruff-fontaine/index.htm.

"Bumps in the Night." *Memphis Flyer Online*. Retrieved 5 February 2008. http://www.memphisflyer.com/memphis/Content?oid = pod:20795.

"Capitol Records." *HauntedHouses.com*. Retrieved 17 January 2008. http://www.hauntedhouses.com/states/tn/capitol_records.cfm.

"Capitol Records Nashville." *Hoover's, Inc*. Retrieved 18 January 2008. http://www.hoovers.com/capitol-nashville/—ID_138930—/free-co-profile.xhtml.

"Capitol Records Nashville Company Profile." *Yahoo! Finance*. Retrieved 18 January 2008. http://biz.yahoo.com/ic/138/138930.html.

"Captain Meriwether Lewis." *PBS.com*. Retrieved 29 January 2008. http://www.pbs.org/lewisandclark/inside/mlewi.html.

"Cemeteries: Factual Information on Mt. Zion & Hopehill." *West Tennessee Ghosthunters*. Retrieved 4 January 2008. http://groups.msn.com/WestTennesseeGhostHunters/cemetaries.msnw?action = get_message . . .

"Cherokee: Cherokee History: Kingsport." *DiscoverKingsport.com*. Retrieved 2 February 2008. http://discoverkingsport.com/h-Cherokee-history.shtml.

"CHERRY-L Archives." *Rootsweb*. Retrieved 2 January 2008. http://archiver.rootsweb.com/th/read/CHERRY/2000-07/0964030512.

"Click Tunnel." *Haunt Master's Club*. Retrieved 20 January 2008. http://www.hauntmastersclub.com/places/sullivan_county_kingsport_click_tunnel.html.

"Creature White Screamer." *The Ultimate MOBILE Collection of the Strange*. Retrieved 3 January 2008. http://mobile.strangeusa.com/viewhaunt.asp?hauntid = 12196.

"Creepy Canines of East Tennessee." *Suite101.com*. Retrieved 4 January 2008. http://www.suite101.com/article.cfm/rottweiler_dogs/104170/3.

"Cumberland Plateau." *Wikipedia*. Retrieved 30 January 2008. http://en.wikipedia.org/wiki/Cumberland_Plateau.

"Cumberland Trail." *Tennessee River Gorge Segment*. Retrieved 30 January 2008. http://www.cumberlandtrail.org/rivergorge.html.

Davidson, Jim. "The Pilgrimage to Elvis Presley's Graceland." *Elvis Symposium 2003-04*. Retrieved 14 December 2007.

"The Death of Meriwether Lewis." *Prairieghosts.com*. Retrieved 29 January 2008. http://www.prairieghosts.com/meriwet.html.

"East Tennessee State University." *Ghosts of the Prairie*. Retrieved 20 January 2008. http://www.prairieghosts.com/etsu.html.

"ETSU 'Ghost' Stories." *Pat's Place*. Retrieved 20 January 2008. http://www.thepat.org/PatPPP15.htm.

"Experience Timeless Traditions and Original Ingenuity." *SoutheastTENNESSEE*. Retrieved 19 February 2008. http://www.southeasttennessee.com/www/doics/20/farm_trail.

"Falcon Manor-B&B at Falcon Rest." *Bed & Breakfast Inns ONLINE*. Retrieved 4 February 2008. http://www.bbonline.com/tn/falcon/.

"Falcon Rest 'New' Name for Historic Falcon Manor." *Falconrest*. Retrieved 5 February 2008. http://www.falconrest.com/namechange.html.

Ferrier, Lindsay. "Fright Night." *Nashville Scene*. Retrieved 3 February 2008. http://www.nashvillescene.com/Stories/Columns/Suburban_Turmoil/2006/11/30/Fright_Night

Fitzhugh, Pat. "The Bell Witch Haunting." *Bellwitch.org*. Retrieved 24 January 2008. http://www.bellwitch.org/story.htm.

Floyd, E. Randall. "Tennessee Bigfoot a Disagreeable Fellow." *Augusta Chronicle*. Retrieved 4 December 2007. http://www.bigfootencounters.com/articles/tennessee.htm.

"Forging Its Own Future." *Smithsonian Magazine*. Retrieved 8 January 2008. http://www.smithsonianmag.com/arts-culture/10021636.html.

"Former Owner's Ghost Haunts Wartrace Hotel?" *Times-Gazette*. Retrieved 4 February 2008. http://www.t-g.com/story/1286155.html.

"Fort Donelson National Battlefield." *The Town of Dover*. Retrieved 29 January 2008. http://www.dovertn.com/area_attractions/index.htm.

"Fort Donelson National Battlefield Park." *GORP*. Retrieved 28 January 2008. http://gorp.away.com/resource/us_nbp/tn?fortd.htm.

"Fort Donelson National Cemetery." *National Park Service*. Retrieved 28 January 2008. http://www.nps.gov/fodo/planyourvisit/fortdonelsonnationalcemetery.htm.

Garland, Ken. "Man's Home Is Castle Built to Stand the Test of Time." *Blountweb.com*. Retrieved 22 January 2008. http://www.blountweb.com/millenniummanor/news03.htm.

"Ghost at the Mansion." *Falconrest*. Retrieved 4 February 2008. http://www.falconrest.com/ghost.htm.

"The Ghost of Clement Hall: Is She Real or Just a Myth?" *University of Tennessee Martin Pacer*. Retrieved 9 February 2008. http://media.www.utmpacer.com/media/storage/paper1175/news/2006/10/31/Features/The- . . .

"Ghostlights." *Obiwan's UFO-Free Paranormal*. Retrieved 14 January 2007. http://www.ghosts.org/ghostlights/ghostlights.html.

"Ghosts of Elvis Presley and Marilyn Monroe Get Married in Graceland." *Weird-websites.com*. 14 December 2007. http://www.weird-websites.com/weird_news/ghosts-Elvis-Presley-Marilyn-Monroe-marr . . .

Bibliography

"The Ghosts of Fiddler's Rock." *The Moonlit Road*. Retrieved 31 December 2007. http://www.themoonlitroad.com/archives/fiddlersrock/fiddlersrock_page001 .html.

"The Ghosts of Graceland: 'The Glass Case.'" *Wirenot.net*. Retrieved 14 December 2007. http://www.wirenot.net/X/Articles/2005/G/ghostsofgraceland.shtml.

"Ghosts of the Ryman Auditorium." *Haunted Tennessee*. Retrieved 28 January 2008. http://www.prairieghosts.com/ryman.html.

"Ghost Stories." *MyOtaku.com*. Retrieved 20 January 2008. http://www.myotaku.com/users/mitzy/posts/906461.

"Graceland." *About.com*. Retrieved 14 December 2007. http://honeymoons.about.com/od/tennessee/a/Graceland.htm.

"Graceland." *Wikipedia*. 14 December 2007. http://en.wikipedia.org/wiki/ Graceland.

"Greenbrier." *Historic Gatlinburg Restaurant*. Retrieved 5 January 2008. http://www.greenbrierrestaurant.com/.

"Greenbrier Restaurant." *Ghosts of Tennessee*. Retrieved 5 January 2008. http://www.tnghost.org/sites/reports/greenbrier_restaurant.html.

"Haunted Magnolia Manor." *Bed & Breakfast Ghost Tours*. Retrieved 5 February 2008. http://www.magnoliamanorbolivartn.com/Ghosts.html.

"Haunted Tennessee." *Prairieghosts.com*. Retrieved 12 February 2008. http://www.prairieghosts.com/haunttn.html.

"Historic Carnton Plantation." *Carnton Plantation History*. Retrieved 30 December 2007. http://www.carnton.org/history.htm.

"Historic Rugby Today." *Rugby Today*. Retrieved 3 February 2008. http://wwww.historicrugby.org/today/today.htm.

"Historic Ryman Auditorium Backstage Guided Tour in Nashville." *Nashvillesight-seeing.com*. Retrieved 24 January 2008. http://www.nashvillesightseeing.com/tours/tourDetail.cfm?tour_id = 9213.

"History & Restoration." *Falconrest*. Retrieved 4 February 2008. http://www.falconrest.com/restoration.htm.

"History of Reelfoot Lake and Lake County." *Reelfoot Chamber*. Retrieved 27 January 2008. http://www.ecsis.net/dsv/lakecounty/reelfoot/ history.html.

"Hunt-Phelan Home Reopens for Business." *Chandler Reports*. Retrieved 11 January 2008. http://www.memphisdailynews.com/Editorial/StoryLead .aspx?id = 90837.

"Hunt-Phelan House." *The Tennessee Encyclopedia of History and Culture*. Retrieved 11 January 2008. http://tennesseeencyclopedia.net/imagegallery .php?EntryID = H091.

"Hunt/Phelan House." *Tennessee.gov*. Retrieved 11 January 2008. http://www.tennesseeanytime.org/homework/historicsites/huntphel.html.

"If Plans Pass Final Muster, Big Changes on Tap at Tennessee Brewery." *Chandler Reports*. Retrieved 31 January 2008. http://www.memphisdailynews.com/Editorial/StoryFocus.aspx?&id = 94719.

"I Love Loretta Lynn's Haunted Plantation home." *I Love This World*. Retrieved 9 February 2008. http://ilovethisworld.com/?p = 1349.

Jordan, Mark. "For Sale? Memphis Could Lose One of Its Most Historic Properties If the Hunt-Phelan Home Heads for the Auction Block." *Memphisflyer.com*. Retrieved 11 January 2008. http://www.memphisflyer.com/backissues/ issues577evr577.htm.

Kimery, Lewis. "The Tennessee Brewery, Memphis TN." *Cohen Congress*. Retrieved 31 January 2008. http://www.lkimeryphoto.com/files/ 47e406a8725911137843e8c01226b409-1.html.

Klein, Mike. "The House That Fear Built." *Blountweb.com*. Retrieved 22 January 2008. http://www.blountweb.com/millenniummanor/news02.htm.

Krist, John. "Lewis & Clark." *Voyage of Rediscovery*. Retrieved 29 January 2008. http://www.voyageofrediscovery.com/part12/trail/index.shtml.

Kuntzelman, Scott G. "Geography of the Sequatchie Valley." *Illinois State University*. Retrieved 19 February 2008. http://www.ilstu.edu/~sgkuntz/research/IntroSequatchie.html.

"The Legend of the Wampus Cat." *Essortment*. Retrieved 4 January 2008. http://ksks.essortment.com/wampuscat_rvmr.htm.

"Long Island Cherokee Kingsport." *DiscoverKingsport.com*. Retrieved 2 February 2008. http://discoverkingsport.com/h-Long-Island.shtml.

"The Long Island Coast." *The Haunted House*. Retrieved 2 February 2008. http://www.care2.com/c2c/groups/disc.html?gpp==3047&pst=1115348&archival=&posts=1.

"Looking for a Good Ghost Story?" *Sheraton Hotels & Resorts*. Retrieved 5 January 2008. http://www.hoteltravelcheck.com/haunted-hotels-chattanooga.html.

"Loretta Lynn's Plantation House." *Loretta Lynn's L&L Dreamspell*. Retrieved 9 February 2008. http://www.lldreamspell.com/LorettaLynns.html.

"Loretta Lynn's Ranch." *Lorettalynn.com*. Retrieved 9 February 2008. http://lorettalynn.com/ranch/.

"Magnolia Manor Ghost Tours." *GooGhoul*. Retrieved 5 February 2008. http://www.googhoul.com/index.cfm/fuseaction/events.viewEventDetails/eventID/1dc5ffd4 . . .

Marsh, D. L. "Ryman Auditorium." *Ghosts of Tennessee*. Retrieved 28 January 2008. http://www.tnghost.org/sites/reports/ryman_auditorium.html.

McNutt, Beth. "ETSU Tops Region's 'Most Haunted' List." *East Tennessean*. Retrieved 20 January 2008. http://media.www.easttennessean.com/media/storage/paper203/news/2001/11/01/News/Ets . . .

McPeak, Alex. "Former U.S. Marine Hospital One of Many 'Paranormal' Places in Memphis." *Dailyhelmsman.com*. Retrieved 8 January 2008. http://media.www.dailyhelmsman.com/media/storage/paper875/news/2004/10/29/News/For . . .

"Memphis Dorm May Host Supernatural Resident." *Dailyhelmsman.com*. Retrieved 14 January 2008. http://media.www.dailyhelmsman.com/media/storage/paper875/news/2006/10/31/News/M . . .

"Millennium Manor Castle." *Blountweb.com*. Retrieved 22 January 2008. http://www.blountweb.com/millenniummanor/.

"The Murder of Meriwether Lewis." *Tennessee History*. Retrieved 29 January 2008. http://www.tennesseehistory.com/class/Meriwether.htm.

"Mynders Hall." *Reslifeweb.memphis.edu*. Retrieved 15 January 2008. http://reslifeweb.memphis.edu/reslife/residencehalls/mynders.asp.

"National Ornamental Metal Museum." *New York Times*. Retrieved 8 January 2008. http://travel.nytimes.com/travel/guides/north-america/united-states/tennessee/memphis/attra . . .

"National Ornamental Metal Museum." *Tennessee Encyclopedia of History and Culture*. Retrieved 8 January 2008. http://tennesseeencyclopedia.net/imagegallery.php?EntryID=NO26.

"Newbury House." *Ghosts of Tennessee*. Retrieved 5 January 2008. http://www.tnghost.org/sites/reports/newbury_house.html.

"No Silence Here." *Knoxnews.com*. Retrieved 22 January 2008. http://blogs.knoxnews.com/knx/silence/archives/2005/05/millennium_mano.shtml.

Bibliography

"Oak Ridge, Tennessee." *Wikipedia*. Retrieved 9 January 2008.
  http://en.wikipedia.org/wiki/Oak_Ridge,_Tennessee.
"Old Gray Cemetery History." *Discoveret.org*. Retrieved 20 January 2008.
  http://www.discoveret.org/oldgray/history.htm.
"The Orpheum." *Orpheum-memphis.com*. Retrieved 1 January 2008.
  http://www.orpheum-memphis.com/index.cfm?page = inside&sub = 1.
"Orpheum Theater." *Cinema Treasures*. Retrieved 2 January 2008. http://
  cinematreasures.org/theater/1679/.
"Orpheum Theatre (Memphis)." *Wikipedia*. Retrieved 1 January 2008.
  http://en.wikipedia.org/wiki/Orpheum_Theatre_(Memphis).
"Overnight Ghost Hunts at Magnolia Manor Bed and Breakfast." *About.com*.
  5 February 2008. http://memphis.about.com/od/thingstoseeanddo/qt/
  magnoliahunts.htm. http://www.geocities.com/elvissymposium/
  davidson.htm.
"Prentice Cooper State Forest Campground." *Trails.com*. Retrieved 30 January
  2008. http://www.trails.com/tcatalog_trail.asp?trailid = HGD170-047.
"Prospect Hill Bed & Breakfast Inn." *Bbonline.com*. Retrieved 7 February 2008.
  http://www.bbonline.com/tn/prespecthill/index.html.
"Prospect Hill Bed & Breakfast Inn." *Prospect-hill.com*. Retrieved 7 February 2008.
  http://www.prospect-hill.com/aboutus.htm.
"The Psychic Experiences of Elvis Presley's Ghost." *The Psychics & Mediums Net-
  work*. Retrieved 14 December 2007.
  http://www.psychics.co.uk/celebrities/elvispresley.html.
"Read House Hotel-Haunted Room 311." *Waymarking.com*. Retrieved 5 January
  2008. http://www.waymarking.com/waymarks/WM23N5.
"Read House: A Part of Chattanooga's History." *American Roads Travel Magazine*.
  Retrieved 7 January 2009. http://www.americanroads.net/ReedHouse.html.
"Reelfoot Lake." *Tennessee.gov*. Retrieved 27 January 2008.
  http://www.tennesseeanytime.org/homework/historicsites/reellake.html
"The Rugby Colony-An Aspiring Utopia." *Historic Rugby*. Retrieved 3 February
  2008. http://www.historicrugby.org/history/history.htm.
Schlosser, S. E. "The Wampus Cat." *American Folklore*. Retrieved 4 January 2008.
  http://www.americanfolklore.net/folktales/tn3.html.
"Sensabaugh Tunnel." *Haunt Masters Club*. Retrieved 20 January 2008.
  http://www.hauntmastersclub.com/places/sullivan_county_kingsport_
  Sensabaugh_tunnel
"Sewanee: The University of the South." *Wikipedia.org*. Retrieved 21 January
  2008. http://en.wikipedia.org/wiki/Sewanee._The_University_of_the_South.
Sublett, Kenneth. "Meriwether Lewis-Lewis County-Hohenwald, Tennessee."
  Piney.2.com. Retrieved 29 January 2008. http://www.piney-2.com/
  DornMLewis.html.
"The Suck Creek Spirit." *The Haunted House*. Retrieved 30 January2008.
  http://www.care2.com/c2c/groups/disc.html?gpp = 3047&pst = 1093331
  &archival = 1.
"Swingle Hospital." *Bridge to the Paranormal*. Retrieved 22 January 2008.
  http://amazingforums.com/forum1/BTTP/101.html.
"Swingle Hospital." *StrangeUSA*. Retrieved 23 January 2008.
  http://www.strangeusa.com/ViewLocation.aspx?locationid = 9245.
"Swingle Hospital, Johnson City, TN." *Urban Exploration Resource*. Retrieved
  22 January 2008. http://www.uer.ca/forum_showthread_archive.asp?fid
  = 1&threadid = 24951&currpage = 1&p . . .
"Tennessee Abductions and UFO Sightings." *BUFO Radio*. Retrieved 17 December
  2007. http://www.burlingtonnews.net/ufotennesseeoakridge.html.

"Tennessee Bigfoot Sightings." *Spacepub.com*. Retrieved 4 December 2007.
   http://www.spacepub.com/users/data/bigfoot/ten/ten.htm.
"Tennessee Bigfoot Video?" *Cryptomundo.com*. Retrieved 4 December 2007.
   http://www.cryptomundo.com/bigfoot-report/tennessee-bigfoot-video/.
"Tennessee High School." *Ghosts of the Prairie*. Retrieved 5 January 2008.
   http://www.prairieghosts.com/bristol.html.
"Tennessee's First Frontier History." *Elizabethon.org*. Retrieved 12 February 2008.
   http://www.elizabethon.org/about/history.html.
"Thomas Hughes." *Historic Rugby*. Retrieved 24 January 2008.
   http://www.historicrugby.org/hughes/hughes.htm.
"The University of Memphis." *Memphis.edu*. Retrieved 15 January 2008.
   http://www.memphis.edu/history.htm.
"UPDATE October 3rd 2006." *Haunted South TV*. Retrieved 20 January 2008.
   http://www.hauntedsouthtv.com/pageDisplay.cfm?CFID = 295342&
   CFTOKEN = 12262723.
"A Virtual History of the University of Tennessee at Martin." *University of
   Tennessee Martin*. Retrieved 9 February 2008. http://www.utm.edu/
   departments/acadpro/library/departments/special_collections/LD5300_ . . .
"Voodoo Village." *Blography of a Southern Writer*. Retrieved 7 January 2009.
   http://blography-of-souther-writer.blogspot.com/2007/01/
   voodoo-village.html.
"Voodoo Village: A Mysterious Little Corner of Haunted Memphis."
   Hauntedamericatours.com. Retrieved 7 January 2008.
   http://www.hauntedamericatours.com/voodoo/voodoovillage/index.php.
"Walking Horse Inn." *Strangeusa.com*. Retrieved 9 February 2008.
   http://www.strangeusa.com/ViewLocation.aspx?locationid = 9349.
"Wampus Cat." *Wikipedia*. Retrieved 4 January 2008.
   http://en.wikipedia.org/wiki/Wampus_cat.
"The Wampus Cat." *Students.ou.edu*. Retrieved 4 January 2008.
   http://students.ou.edu/M/Callie.L.Miller-1/callies%20cat.html.
"Welcome to Hurricane Mills." *Loretta Lynn Fan*. Retrieved 9 February 2008.
   http://www.lorettalynnfan.com/hurricanemillstn.htm.
"Welcome to Magnolia Manor Bed & Breakfast." *Magnoliamanorbolivartn.com*.
   Retrieved 5 February 2008. http://www.magnoliamanorbolivartn.com/
   index.html.
"White Bluff Legends & Tales from the Campfire." *White Bluff, Tennessee Area
   Legends, Lies and Ghost Stories*. Retrieved 3 January 2008. http://members
   .tripod.com/ ~ blufwatch/wblegends.html.
Williams, Kathy Riley. "Rugby, Tennessee: A Place Apart." *Southern Scribe*.
   Retrieved 3 February 2008. http://www.southernscribe.com/zine/
   landmarks/Rugby_TN.htm.
"Witchcraft." *Wikipedia*. Retrieved 24 January 2008.
   http://en.wikipedia.org/wiki/Witchcraft.

Acknowledgments

I THANK MICHAEL ESPANJER, DIRECTOR OF MEMPHIS PARANORMAL Research Team, for sharing his group's experiences in the haunted places of Memphis. I also thank Dr. James Gentsch and Dustin Prine of the University of West Alabama for assisting me with the section of the ghosts of Shiloh. Thanks also go to the University Research Committee at UWA for providing me with the funding for my research. I am also grateful to Troy Taylor, whose research on the Civil War ghosts of Tennessee has really enhanced the quality of this book. And of course, the publication of *Haunted Tennessee* would not have been possible without the assistance and invaluable contributions of artist Heather Adel Wiggins and Kyle Weaver and Brett Keener at Stackpole Books.

About the Author

ALAN BROWN IS A PROFESSOR OF ENGLISH AT THE UNIVERSITY OF WEST Alabama in Livingston. Brown has written extensively about the folklore of Alabama and the rest of the South as well. His interest in southern ghost stories led him to write *Haunted Places in the American South, Stories from the Haunted South, Ghost Hunters of the South, Haunted Georgia,* and *Haunted Texas.* When he is not teaching or writing, Brown gives ghost tours of the city of Livingston and UWA's campus.

CPSIA information can be obtained
at www.ICGtesting.com
Printed in the USA
BVHW070321290821
615080BV00001B/4

9 780811 735407